Still Moving

Still Moving

The Journey of Love's Perfection

Robert C. Pelfrey

RESOURCE *Publications* • Eugene, Oregon

STILL MOVING
The Journey of Love's Perfection

Copyright © 2017 Robert C. Pelfrey. All rights reserved. Except for brief quotations in critical publications or reviews, no part of this book may be reproduced in any manner without prior written permission from the publisher. Write: Permissions, Wipf and Stock Publishers, 199 W. 8th Ave., Suite 3, Eugene, OR 97401.

Resource Publications
An Imprint of Wipf and Stock Publishers
199 W. 8th Ave., Suite 3
Eugene, OR 97401

www.wipfandstock.com

PAPERBACK ISBN: 978-1-5326-3001-9
HARDCOVER ISBN: 978-1-5326-3003-3
EBOOK ISBN: 978-1-5326-3002-6

All Scripture quotations, unless otherwise indicated, are taken from the Holy Bible, *New International Version*®, NIV®. Copyright ©1973, 1978, 1984, 2011 by Biblica, Inc.™ Used by permission of Zondervan. All rights reserved worldwide. www.zondervan.com The "NIV" and "New International Version" are trademarks registered in the United States Patent and Trademark Office by Biblica, Inc.™

Scripture quotations designated "NRSV" are from the *New Revised Standard Version*, copyright © 1989 National Council of the Churches of Christ in the United States of America. Used by permission. All rights reserved worldwide.

Scripture quotations designated "NLT" are from the Holy Bible, *New Living Translation*, copyright ©1996, 2004, 2007, 2013, 2015 by Tyndale House Foundation. Used by permission of Tyndale House Publishers, Inc., Carol Stream, Illinois 60188. All rights reserved.

Manufactured in the U.S.A.

To my mother, Betty Jane Lemons Pelfrey,
a model of love's perfection.

Contents

Acknowledgments | xi

Introduction: A Strange Account of Christian Perfection | xiii

PART I
Heart: Where There's a Will

1. Crashing | 3
2. The Power to Become, or How to Fight with a Preschooler | 8
3. It Was Like That When I Got Here | 15
4. The Plot Thickens | 19

   Steps on the Journey:
   Learning to Love with Your Whole Heart | 23

PART II
Mind: The Story You Find Yourself In

5. Learning God's Story | 27
6. Living God's Story | 31
7. Learning Your Story | 36
8. Living Your Story | 50

   Steps on the Journey:
   Learning to Love with Your Whole Mind | 57

CONTENTS

PART III
Strength: Brute Beauty

9   Mirror, Mirror | 61

10 The King is Dead | 66

11 The Power of the Temple, or How to Get Punched Out | 70

12 Armchair Quarterbacks | 78

    Steps on the Journey:
    Learning to Love with Your Whole Strength | 82

PART IV
Soul: Deep Like Rivers

13 Take Me to the River | 87

14 Robert Johnson's Deal | 90

15 Possessed | 94

16 The Power of Letting Go, or How to Get Away from a Tiger | 100

    Steps on the Journey:
    Learning to Love with Your Whole Soul | 105

PART V
Neighbors: Walling In or Walling Out

17 Across the Tracks | 109

    Steps on the Journey:
    Tearing Down Walls of Prejudice | 114

18 Royalty | 116

    Steps on the Journey:
    Tearing Down Walls of Class | 119

19 The Power of Life, or How to Get Away with Murder | 120

CONTENTS

    Steps on the Journey:
    Tearing Down Walls of Violence | 123

20 With God on Our Side | 125

    Steps on the Journey:
    Tearing Down Walls of Ideology | 129

    Conclusion: Becoming the Land | 130

Acknowledgments

I developed much of the material for this project as pastor among the dear brothers and sisters of Western Hills United Methodist Church in El Paso, Texas. They are blessed and they are a blessing because they have a hunger and thirst for righteousness and an insatiable appetite for God's word.

The team at Wipf and Stock has been a pleasure to collaborate with. They are doing good, important work, and I am grateful to be part of it.

Daniel Harris is a beloved friend and teacher whose vocation as a spiritual director continually spills over into my life, offering refreshment and nourishment. His contributions to the "Steps on the Journey" sections were invaluable.

My own journey of love's perfection is shared with family and friends that are constant means of God's grace in my life. My wife, Jamie, and our daughter, Maddie Jane, continue to teach me about love in surprising, challenging, and hilarious ways. I could survey the world and not find better companions for the journey.

Introduction

A Strange Account of Christian Perfection

We all face those questions, the kinds of questions that change a life. They're much bigger than the everyday, paper-or-plastic, do-you-want-fries-with-that questions. Will you follow Jesus? What do you want to do with your life? Will you marry me? Do you want the job? What are we going to do about our kids? And so on.

There's one such series of questions that I believe should be taken as seriously as those others. People in my line of work have to answer them in front of our peers, mentors, and authority figures. I answered them a number of years ago. I stood there, hundreds of pairs of eyes staring at me, friends and strangers waiting for me to answer. I was sweating a little. My face flushed. My heart thumped in my ears. My eyes glazed and everything dimmed into one big blur of anxiety. Behind me were scores of pastors, from relative newbies like me, to the dynamic leaders of dynamic churches, to wise and scrutinizing retirees. In front of me was the bishop, who stood on a stage as I stood on the floor facing him, facing his questions.

I was being examined by the bishop, asked the same questions Methodist clergy had been asked for generations. Then my fellow pastors would vote to approve my ordination . . . or not. A number of questions are asked. They're mostly things you might expect pertaining to the rules and doctrines of the church, instructing the children, commitment to the work of God, and the like. All are to be considered carefully and committed to humbly. But right at the beginning, after "Have you faith in Christ?" (hardly a throwaway question), are perhaps the most intimidating and, for many, the most misunderstood and underappreciated questions.

INTRODUCTION

"Are you going on to perfection?"
"Do you expect to be made perfect in love in this life?"
"Are you earnestly striving after it?"[1]

Some pastors don't take these questions so seriously. Some see this penultimate stage in the ordination process as a mere formality. But many (hopefully most) of us feel what can only be described as a divine weight on our shoulders in this moment. *Am I going on to perfection? Do I really expect to be made perfect in love in this life? Am I earnestly striving after it? Earnestly?* As each of these questions came to me from the bishop I felt myself floating in a river with generations—generations of pastors who had answered these questions and preached these truths before me, some of whom had been my pastors; generations of theologians who had worked to understand and teach this doctrine of Christian perfection, some of whom had been my professors; generations of laypeople who had struggled with and earnestly striven after this perfection, some of whom were my own family. Now the questions were asked of me. My throat was dry as I answered.

This stuff of Christian perfection seems strange to many, even many in the family of denominations in which it has been most explicitly embraced. But it shouldn't be strange to any disciple of Jesus Christ. And it certainly isn't to be relegated to certain denominations. It's as broad as Jesus's words, "Be perfect, therefore, as your heavenly Father is perfect" (Matt 5:48). But perfect? Nobody's perfect. Why does Jesus say this? Was he setting us up for failure? Was he joking? Is this just some fringe fixation of a specific branch in the Christian family tree? Or just maybe, was Jesus expecting more of us—and promising more *to* us—than we are willing to accept? As C.S. Lewis noted, "[Jesus] never talked vague, idealistic gas. When He said, 'Be perfect,' He meant it. He meant that we must go in for the full treatment . . . We are like eggs at present. And you cannot go on indefinitely being just an ordinary, decent egg. We must be hatched or go bad."[2]

This is a book about hatching. This is not a book about the doctrine of Christian perfection *per se*. I won't be going to great lengths to explain or defend it as a doctrine. However, there is a vital understanding about the nature of this perfection we need to come to before we continue: Christian perfection is the work of God's grace, and it is defined in God's love. Jesus,

1. *Discipline*, 262.
2. Lewis, *Mere Christianity*, 169.

INTRODUCTION

in the above admonition to "be perfect," is concluding his famous words about loving everyone, including one's enemies. And these words are part of the Sermon on the Mount—a picture of the blessed life found in Jesus's company and lordship. But what sort of love is this? What sort of life is this?

In the first century and first years of the church, the apostle Paul pronounced this very optimistic blessing: "May the God of peace himself sanctify you entirely; and may your spirit and soul and body be kept sound and blameless at the coming of our Lord Jesus Christ. The one who calls you is faithful, and he will do this" (1 Thess 5:23–24, NRSV). Another term often associated with Christian perfection is "entire sanctification," based on this passage. To be sanctified entirely is to be completely set apart *from* sin and *for* abundant life in Christ. Again we are tempted to wonder, Is Paul joking? Your spirit and soul and body kept sound and blameless? The key, of course, is the affirmation, "The one who calls you is faithful, and *he* will do this." This is about God's power, not ours.

The writer of the letter to the Hebrews urged the persecuted first-century Christians, "Therefore let us go on toward perfection, leaving behind the basic teaching about Christ . . . " (6:1, NRSV). This is the source of that ordination question, asking if we pastors are actually doing this. The Greek for "perfection" here (*teleiotēs*) is rooted in the image of reaching a goal, hence the admonition to "go on toward" and "strive after" this perfection. Don't stop with the basics. That would be like thinking the point of a race is just to get off the starting line. Keep going! The idea of perfection and of running toward a goal is big in Hebrews. But strive as we must, the author reminds us that "we will do this [reach the goal], *if God permits*" (6:3, my emphasis). Once again, this goal is not reached solely on our own merits.

Another letter written to those first Christians (and one of the most beautiful and important sections in all of holy scripture) is the epistle 1 John. In it the wise apostle explains perfection in terms of the intertwining of obedience and the love of God. He explains, "[W]hoever obeys [God's] word, truly in this person the love of God has reached perfection," and, "There is no fear in love, but perfect love casts out fear; for fear has to do with punishment, and whoever fears has not reached perfection in love" (1 John 2:5 and 4:18, NRSV). So it is God's love that brings us to perfection, and especially our participation in God's love. Once again the onus of perfection is on God but requires our loving response, as John masterfully explains, "We love because he first loved us" (4:19).

INTRODUCTION

In the second century, Irenaeus of Lyons wrote, "The glory of God is humanity fully alive, and life consists in beholding God."[3] What is it to be fully alive? What does this look and feel like? I have a hunch it's more than the old Romantic ideal of *carpe diem*. The path of this life lies in nothing less than beholding the God who is love. This "beholding" is more than a fleeting glimpse. This idea of being fully alive is bound up in growing toward maturity in love, and thus it is bound up in perfection. Life itself is beholding God. So perfection for Irenaeus was *fully* beholding God, which is to say beholding God in every part of our being. And again, we are not the source of this life, but it is God's glory and God who is beheld.

Later (and, for the sake of brevity, bypassing many great teachers), in the fourteenth century, mystic teacher John of Ruusbroec wrote about "the common life," a life of simultaneously flowing inward with love toward God, resting in God's love, and flowing outward with love toward others. He wrote, "A person who has been sent down by God from these heights [of mystic contemplation] into the world is full of truth and rich in all the virtues. He seeks nothing of his own but only the glory of the one who sent him . . . He therefore leads a common life, for he is equally ready for contemplation or for action and is perfect in both."[4] Perfect in contemplation and action is akin to Irenaeus's fully beholding (contemplation) and being fully alive (action). And for Ruusbroec it is all about being one with God in the inward and outward flow of love.

In the sixteenth century in her *The Way of Perfection*, Teresa of Avila wrote of a way of living prayer that included love of neighbor, detachment from worldliness and self, and humility in receiving all of life as a gift from God. She wrote, "May the Lord, because of who He is, give us the grace to seek this living water as it should be sought, for He promises it."[5] Teresa calls this prayerful, holistic life of love, detachment, and humility "the way of perfection." And it depends on the Lord's character and promises. Only by God's grace may we drink deeply of the living water, of which God is the source.

In the eighteenth century in his *A Plain Account of Christian Perfection*, John Wesley explained, "What is Christian perfection? The loving God with all our heart, mind, soul, and strength. This implies that no wrong temper, none contrary to love, remains in the soul; and that all the

---

3. Irenaeus, *Heresies* IV, 20:7, 425.
4. Ruusbroec, *Espousals*, 184.
5. Teresa of Avila, *Perfection* 19.2, 113.

INTRODUCTION

thoughts, words and actions, are governed by pure love."[6] And so we come full circle back to the master, Jesus, and a life of all-encompassing love.

In each of these examples of teaching on Christian perfection (and these only scratch the surface), we should notice the origin of this perfect love: it comes from God. Christian perfection is not about being (in the words of Al Franken's Stuart Smalley) "good enough, smart enough, and doggonit, people like me." It is not about being self-actualized or having life so together that one has "arrived." Rather, Christian perfection is only the result of the grace of God working in the life of the one earnestly striving after it, striving after God. And it is grounded in, and bears the fruit of, love. That's where this perfection is found—where our swimming is picked up and carried on by the strong current of God's grace.[7]

And that's what I had in mind when I answered each of my ordination questions. I knew this idea of perfection did not mean I'd never again make mistakes, that I'd never again get sick or suffer or experience the ramifications of sin (mine or others'), or even that I'd never again sin, whether unknowingly or by willfully resisting God's grace. I just knew it was a pledge to take Jesus at his word, that God's plan is for me to love completely, perfectly. And that God will give me the grace to be perfected in love as God's love is perfected in me.

So I answered: "Yes, in God's grace, I am going on to perfection. Yes, in God's grace, I expect to be made perfect in love in this life. Yes, in God's powerful, purposeful, perfect and perfecting grace, I am striving after this perfection, this complete love." Otherwise, what's the point? Are we serious about this love business, or aren't we? I actually think these questions would be good to include in church membership vows. They should not only be asked of potential pastors but are appropriate for any potential church member, even anyone making the decision to follow Jesus. We are each and all called to maturity in Christlikeness. And that's what we're really talking about with perfection. There is much to explore, consider, and even debate in this concept, most of which I will *not* do here. There are many good works out there devoted to the topic.[8] What I want to focus on is love . . . total, complete, perfect love. It is enough. It's all you need (at least

---

6. Wesley, *Plain Account*, 51.

7. For an excellent resource on the role of God's grace in Christian maturity and perfection, see Harris, *Grace that Grows*.

8. See, for example, the edition of *Plain Account* edited, annotated, and introduced by Chilcote and Maddox. See also the variety of perspectives in works like Marin's *The Theology of Christian Perfection* and Colon-Emeric's *Wesley, Aquinas and Christian Perfection*.

according to The Beatles). So that's what I want to explore. More, it is what I want to *do*. Who besides a total psychopath is going to argue with that?

As Wesley concluded, "Now let this perfection appear in its native form, and who can speak one word against it? Will any dare to speak against loving the Lord our God with all our heart, and our neighbors as ourselves? . . . or against having all the mind that was in Christ, and walking in all things as Christ walked? What person, who calls themselves a Christian, has the hardiness to object to the devoting, not a part, but all our soul, body, and substance to God?"[9] Despite many times in which my attitude and actions make it seem as if I *do* object to this complete devotion of love, it is indeed what I'm about. This is the journey I'm on. I imagine we're on it together.

There is inherent in these questions—of being made perfect in love in this life and striving after it—a dual movement. The question "Do you expect to *be made perfect* in love in this life?" sounds passive. And, to a large degree, it is. It is God's work, not mine. I cannot make myself love God or others perfectly any more than I can make the sun come up in the morning. But I can face east and open my curtains. And that gets at the other question: "Are you *earnestly striving* after it?" There are things I can do to receive this love, to rest and trust in this love, to selflessly and sacrificially share this love . . . to participate in this love. That's the better way of putting it, to "participate in the divine nature" (2 Pet 1:4). That, in the end, is what we're striving after: participating in the love, the life, and the very nature of the God who is love. We strive after what God is freely offering. We love because God first loved us.

That is the reason for this book's title, *Still Moving*. This is the dual posture of perfect love. First, we are still—resting and trusting in God's grace and allowing ourselves to come to know love and to be loved. We are *being made* perfect in love. And second (though simultaneously), we are moving—training to become lovers and flowing inward and outward with God's perfect love. We are *earnestly striving* after love's perfection. Living in this balance—sometimes a bitter dissonance, sometimes a sweet harmony—is the completion, the perfection of love: still, moving. A key insight into the nature of this love, however, is that it is never static. It is complete in the sense of being whole, but not in the sense of being finished. We might be who we are meant to be right now, free from sin and free to love. But we are not who we will one day be, not even who we will be next

---

9. Wesley, *Plain Account*, 118, language slightly updated.

INTRODUCTION

year, much less in the eternal ages of ages. The journey of love's perfection never ends. But we must begin.

So, following Wesley and others as they point to Jesus, we'll consider this idea of earnestly striving toward being made perfect in love in this life in terms of wholly loving God and wholly loving our neighbors. The book is divided into five parts: Heart, Mind, Strength, Soul, and Neighbors. Each part consists of four chapters. The first four parts explore what it is to love God completely by exploring the vital aspects of ourselves, including our being in God and in God's great universe. The fifth part turns us outward toward our neighbors, with an emphasis on tearing down personal and societal walls that divide us: prejudice, class, violence, and ideology. This section on loving our neighbors is only a start, yet the attentive reader will see an emphasis on the outward expression of love, the building of community, and the transformation of culture and the world in every chapter of the first four parts.

Indeed, all of this is merely a beginning. Jesus goes to the trouble of qualifying the nature of this love by emphasizing wholeness in each aspect of our being. Love God with your *whole* heart, your *whole* mind, your *whole* strength, and your *whole* soul. Identifying and integrating and nurturing and maturing a wholly loving self—all while yielding to and cooperating with God's grace—is an eternal proposition. And being transformed by and into the kind of love that wholly embraces others, including one's enemies, only adds to the challenge of the journey. To help us along the way, I've followed each of the first four parts with a section called "Steps on the Journey," which contains scriptures and questions for consideration and discussion, as well as actions for deeper exploration and development. Because each of the four chapters in the Neighbors section deals with a different topic, I've followed each chapter with "Steps on the Journey." Through it all, we will learn to be still and to move . . . sometimes one or the other, but often simultaneously. So let's get going. To paraphrase Confucius, the journey of love's perfection begins with the first step.

PART I

Heart: Where There's a Will

1

Crashing

You never forget your first car crash. My friend Thomas lived in a house that was perched on the rim of a canyon. It was in a gated community about fifteen miles outside of the town I lived in. The gate was a high cyclone fence with barbed wire across the top, like some sort of cult compound, and the gate slid open electronically when either a key-card was inserted or when someone rolled over a sensor in the ground on the inside. What this meant was that a person had one of three options to enter: have a key-card; pull over and wait, hoping a random car came along and opened the gate either with a key card or exiting from the inside; or arrange ahead of time (these were the days before the proliferation of cell-phones) for someone to meet you at the gate.

In high school and college my friends and I often hung out together all night. Early one Saturday morning, after one of those Friday all-nighters, I was taking Thomas back to his home out in the gated canyon. The first salmon and orange rays of the sun were emerging on the horizon. As we turned off the main road and headed down the couple-mile-long stretch toward the gate, Thomas realized he'd forgotten his gate key. We spotted in the distance that the gate was still open from a car that had just pulled through.

"You can make it," Thomas said. "Punch it!" (We used to say things like that.)

I hit the gas in my big Oldsmobile and we sped toward the gate, which was now beginning to close. Adrenaline pumped as the opening narrowed.

"Never mind, Robert," Thomas said firmly. I only sped up. "Forget it, man," he shouted, "you can't make it!"

At the last second I stomped on the brake. We skidded through as the gate crashed into Thomas's side of the car, sending broken glass all over the guy, who had turned pale with shock. We slid off the road—on the *inside* of the gate, thank you very much—and sat there for a minute. I asked Thomas if he was okay. He was, besides the pellets of glass he would spend the next several days washing out of his long hair. But we got inside that gate. I wish I could say it was the last time I crashed my way where I wanted to go.

Where are you heading? How are you getting there? You might have a plan and you might not. Maybe you go with the flow, letting circumstances dictate your path. Or maybe you're driven by a desire to achieve and you have a detailed roadmap to success. You might have a key or you might be speeding toward a closing gate. Perhaps you have people encouraging you to "Punch it!" And perhaps you have people telling you to forget it. (And maybe it's the same people saying both.) But in the end, *you're* driving. So what's driving you?

Think about that while I introduce you to some people I've encountered. Perhaps you've met some of them too. (The names have, of course, been changed.)

Here's James. James wants to be rich. He eagerly admits this. He works non-stop, killing himself to impress his bosses, spending weekends attending conferences and golfing with clients. He invests and keeps an obsessive watch on the markets. He's even started cutting some corners and getting creative with his taxes and finances. And it's working—James has lots of money. James also has a wife, an eight-year-old son, and a three-year-old daughter. James promises his family he'll spend some time with them just as soon as things settle down at work.

Marie likes to have a good time. She enjoys good food, relaxing vacations, and parties. If it feels good, do it! After work most days Marie meets friends at a local bar. Sometimes she has a little too much to drink, even blacking out occasionally on weekends. But she handles it okay. She likes to be pampered, so she moves from relationship to relationship—they're always the most fun at the beginning. She knows if she can meet the right guy they'll settle down and live the good life. In the meantime, she's just having fun. Marie once joked to me that she's "an advocate for life, liberty, and the pursuit of happiness . . . especially the happiness part."

Steve is the boss. Steve has always been the boss, even as a kid. After college he kept his nose to the grindstone and eventually became the head of an exciting and profitable company. He runs a tight ship with no real room for employee input or criticism. After all, he's the boss and he knows best. And he has the awards and influence to prove it. He runs his family the same way. His wife and three kids always look like a picture, and with only a glance he can get them all in line. He's the envy of his colleagues, and if he had any real friends they'd probably be jealous of him too.

Of course there's much more to James, Marie, and Steve than these brief descriptions. But what we have here are snapshots—snapshots of the human heart. These folks and many like them are driven by the classic pursuits: money, pleasure, and power. Maybe you identify with one of these people. I've been each of them at one time or another, and probably could be again. So, is there anything wrong with these pursuits? Anything wrong with making a good living, having a good time, being in charge? No, not really. On the contrary, money and pleasure and power can be part of a healthy life, even a godly life. It's when they have your heart that you're in trouble.

Jesus said, "Show me your treasure and I'll show you your heart."[1] So what does this mean? What kind of heart is Jesus talking about? The blood-pumping muscle in the middle of your chest? Your emotions and feelings, especially romantic feelings? Or is the heart something more, maybe much more? Jesus said the greatest commandment a human can follow is (in part) to "love the Lord your God with all your heart" (Mark 12:30). This seems like pretty big stuff—more than just a bodily organ or fleeting feelings. So what is this heart?

In a word, your heart is your *will*. It's the core of your being in the sense that it's what drives you, what you're really about. Your heart is also a significant part of what is meant when the Bible talks about your spirit, because while your will is currently lived out in and affected by your body, it is not restricted to your body. Your heart is spiritual. Beyond biology, genetics, or cultural constructs, you heart is a big part of what makes you *you*.[2] So, this being the case, your heart is also what God looks at when God considers you. As God revealed to the prophet Samuel, "The Lord does not look at the things human beings look at. People look at the outward appearance, but the Lord looks at the heart" (1 Sam 16:7). When God considers you, God is not looking at your body or your clothes, not at the polish and production value with which you try so hard to impress others. God looks

---

1. See Matthew 6:21. I've adapted Wright's translation: "Show me your treasure, and I'll show you where your heart is." Wright, *Kingdom*, 10.

2. In describing the will/heart/spirit, Willard uses helpful phrases like "the capacity for *radical* and *underivative* origination of events and things" and "the core of our non-physical being," as well as "the executive center of the human self [from which] the whole self or life is meant to be directed and organized." Willard, *Renovation*, 144.

at your heart, at the core of your being, what it is you will throughout your life. In some ways this might be a relief. In other ways it might be a problem.

"Show me your treasure and I'll show you your heart," says Jesus. Show me your goals, your values, how you spend your time, how you define success, and I'll show you what drives you, where you're heading, and who you really are. Many of these aspects of the heart might come to us providentially, through upbringing and circumstances. But the formation of the heart is also the result of choices, and ever more so as we mature. Plenty of people come from the darkest of upbringings and direst of circumstances, yet they form a heart of gold. Likewise, many experience a solid upbringing and ideal circumstances, yet their heart is gray and withered from lack of light. Each of us has a will. Made in the image of the Creator, we too are creators. We can't create from nothing, so perhaps something like "shapers" is more accurate. But we are given this heart, this will, this spirit-life, not from our parents or from society. It is a gift from God alone. It is God's "breath" in us—not breath in the way we think of it, but part of our God-given aliveness.[3] And we can do with it as we please.

You can use your will to pursue money. You can even tell yourself you're doing it for others. You can use your will to pursue pleasure. You can even call it the good life. You can use your will to pursue power. You can even call it the American dream. Each new day you are exercising your will, driving through life in this body with your heart giving the directions. So I ask again, Where are you heading?

Matt wants to make a difference. He's a lawyer who works mostly for justice on behalf of the poor. He makes a modest living, but it's enough to provide for his family and to give some away. He likes to spend his time doing anything or nothing with his family. They are active in their church. They host a small group Bible study in their home. Matt mentors a young law student named Josh. They get together every week—have coffee, play golf occasionally, sometimes Josh has dinner or goes to church with Matt's family. They don't talk much about religion. But upon graduation, there are two big lessons Josh tells me he has learned from Matt: one, happiness and peace come from knowing what you're about (and what you're not about); and two, success comes from being about what God is about.

---

3. For an excellent exploration of the concept of "spirit," including its connection with the breath of life, see Levison, *Fresh Air*.

So, what are you about? Spend some time listening to your heart—not just the beating in your chest or how you feel, but considering your will. What is this life you are making, this world you are creating? Maybe you didn't realize you have a will, a heart, a spirit. Maybe you thought your life was the result of circumstances beyond your control. You're just playing the hand you were dealt, just getting by. Or you're caught up in the cultural current, being pulled along by dreams of money, pleasure, and/or power.

Now, in light of this consideration, set aside a few minutes, grab a pen and a piece of paper, and do this fun exercise. You don't necessarily need to share this with anyone else. Hide or throw away the paper when you're done. This is just for you.

In the publishing and movie businesses there's something called the logline or one-line, also known as the elevator pitch (i.e. you're on an elevator with a big shot executive and you have a one-floor ride to sell your story). This would be a compelling one-sentence description of what the story is about. Some examples would be:

Star Wars: Episode IV—"A farm boy longing for adventure joins a band of rebels, trains as a mystical knight with special powers, and cripples an evil empire."

Disney's *The Lion King*—"A loose adaptation of *Hamlet* in which a young lion prince flees his kingly destiny after his father dies, and must find the courage to confront the uncle who killed his father and to lead the animal kingdom."

Cormac McCarthy's *No Country for Old Men*—"A cowboy discovers the scene of a drug deal gone wrong, takes a suitcase filled with money, and flees a psychopathic killer seeking to claim the money."

Now you. Write an elevator pitch for your life story. It doesn't need to include your life up to this point (though it can). But focus on your life from this point on. You've written a story at the end of this coming year of your life. Or at the end of the coming ten years. Or at the end of the coming fifty years. But you've come to the end of this period, written a story about it, and you have one sentence to pitch it to a big shot on an elevator. Go.

2

The Power to Become, or How to Fight with a Preschooler

Years later I can recall the moment like it was last night. It's frozen in time. It wasn't a tragedy, but I can even imagine the lighting and the emotion . . . definitely the emotion. My four-year-old daughter had done something wrong (of course I don't remember what it was, which is a lesson in itself). It was bedtime, which typically resulted in a struggle of wills that was problematic enough. I was scolding her, speaking firmly, strongly. Okay, I was yelling. She sat in her bed smiling at me, her big brown eyes gazing adoringly at me. This made me even angrier.

"This isn't funny," I insisted. I continued my lecture and she continued smiling. I towered over her, gesticulating wildly, and I suppose expecting complex reasoning and profound contrition from my tiny, curly-haired preschooler. She simply smiled.

I finally demanded, "What are you smiling at?"

"I'm just smiling cuz I love you," she said.

Silence. My eyes glazed with tears. Needless to say, that ended the one-sided argument. And needless to say, I lost. Outsmarted by a four-year-old. (I wish it was the only time.) Love has a way of cutting through our self-importance and self-righteousness and striking right at the heart, reminding us who we are and what's really important. But unlike the Hollywood and Hallmark idea of love that dominates our culture—the idea that love is something we "fall in" like a big hole in the ground and, conveniently, "fall out of" when we no longer have the warm-fuzzies—love must be chosen. We can't count on a curly-haired cutie to let fly an arrow of adoration at our heart and snap us out of our delusions of grandeur. Love must be chosen, worked for, fought for. Love must be willed.

Let's go back to the beginning . . . the very beginning. Adam and Eve had a choice: to eat the forbidden fruit or not to eat the forbidden fruit. The serpent tempted them with it, they ate it, God found out and got angry and kicked them out of the garden. Right? That's pretty much the way most people—including many Christians—think of the story. As a result, we think of free will in terms of a similar choice: obey God for a reward or disobey God for punishment. This is where we get our moralistic, legalistic, do's-and-don'ts approach to faith. And the heart has very little to do with it.

But Adam and Eve could have totally avoided the tree they were told not to eat from and still broken their relationship with God. The issue wasn't just that they disobeyed God. It was much deeper than that. Adam and Eve had a heart issue. Humans have always had a heart issue. This is the problem from the beginning and across the ages. Listen to Jesus quoting Isaiah: "These people honor me with their lips, but their hearts are far from me" (Matt 15:8; see Isa 29:13). God sees through flattery and empty obedience. God sees through it right to the wayward heart. And what is it God wants from the heart? Intimacy, faithfulness, love. The sin of Adam and Eve wasn't just in their actions; it was in their hearts.

Here's my version of the real story (more or less). The world was created as a temple of the Creator, a sacred place where creation praises its maker in the very act of its being and flourishing. This Creator brought forth humans among creation, creatures made in the image of the Creator with their own power to create (or perhaps more accurately, to cultivate), which we call free will. They were given dominion over creation, God's gracious blessing to work alongside the Creator to help make the creation flourish. As they lived in intimate relationship with each other, with their Maker-Father, and with creation, they would grow and mature and lead the earth toward growth and maturity.

But with their power to create, their free will, they were allowed to do things on their own if they chose to, which they did. It wasn't just that they disobeyed God by eating from the one tree God told them not to eat from. It was that (now lean in close for this), instead of being co-creators alongside the Creator with dominion over creation, they subjected themselves to that creation, to a creature, the serpent. And instead of trusting the Father's grace to lead them naturally and gradually toward growth and maturity, they went on their own and took a shortcut. That's the subtlety of the sin. Adam and Eve were seeking to fulfill their God-given destiny—to bear the image and likeness of God—but to do it *without God*. That's the temptation as the serpent presents it: When you eat from the tree you will be like God (see Gen 3:5). So the original sin was not that our first parents disobeyed a stern, forbidding God and got us all in trouble. It was that they chose to follow their hearts in a direction that led them away from the intimate, faithful, loving union with the Father for which they were made.[1]

And so the struggle continues with us. We have free will like Adam and Eve had. It is, after all, the story of each of us, at least to the extent that we still live in this covenant as creatures created by this gracious Creator. We can trust the care of our Creator. Or we can submit ourselves to the creation, trusting various forms of money, pleasure, and power. We can grow and mature in, and by, the grace of God. Or we can seek one shortcut after another, following the so-called "wisdom" of celebrities, self-help gurus, and our own egos. We can fulfill our destiny of being like God by denying ourselves, taking up our cross, and following Jesus Christ toward loving, faithful intimacy with the Father. Or we can strive after godlikeness through self-aggrandizement. In short, we can turn our hearts toward pursuing union with God, or not.

Each day we walk through life exercising our own free will. Whether we're surrounded by farms or an urban jungle, we move like Adam and Eve in the garden, entrusting our hearts to the Creator or to the creation. But be sure, it's about the heart. By the time Adam and Eve actually disobeyed God and ate the forbidden fruit, I suspect their hearts were long gone. Jesus gave us a great pair of images (see Matt 12:33–35). First, in keeping with the Adam and Eve theme, Jesus talks about trees and fruit. Grow a healthy tree and get healthy fruit. Grow a rotten tree and get rotten fruit. But the fruit is just the product of the tree. And second, Jesus talks about treasure. Valuable riches come from a treasure chest filled with real treasure. Junk riches come from a treasure chest filled with counterfeit treasure. But the treasure that's presented comes from what's in the chest.

The obvious point is that it's what's inside that counts. A healthy, rich heart produces a healthy, rich life. But the less obvious point is where the

---

1. Brueggemann explains, "The freedom of creation is taken seriously by the creator. Therefore, his sovereign rule is expressed in terms of faithfulness, patience, and anguish." He further notes that the creation exists "only because of and for the sake of the creator's purpose," and "the response of creation to creator is a mixture of faithful obedience and recalcitrant self-assertion." Brueggemann, *Genesis*, 13.

responsibility lies. Jesus says *grow* a healthy tree or *grow* an unhealthy tree and you'll get healthy or unhealthy fruit. And then, the good or evil person produces good or evil treasure out of the good or evil *stored up* within them. The health of our tree and the wealth of our treasure depend on us—what kind of heart we're forming, how we exercise our free will.

How might Adam and Eve's story have gone? They could've said to the creature and its empty promise of self-fulfilling godlikeness, "Real life doesn't come from this fruit, but by communing with God. We will not test God. We are committed to worshiping our God and serving only him." These, of course, were the responses of Jesus, the new Adam, when confronted with the tempter and the same temptations to seek shortcuts and self-aggrandizement and creature-worship rather than remain faithful to the Father (see Matt 4:1–10). Interestingly, Jesus went on to accomplish each of the things to which he was tempted—miraculously producing bread (John 6:1–11), being attended to by angels (Matt 4:11; Luke 22:43), becoming king of heaven and earth (Matt 28:18). But all of these were done as a result of his heart's total commitment to the Father. But like Adam and Eve's story, Jesus's story could have gone a different direction.

And your story can go different directions. You can choose what kind of tree you're growing. You can choose what kind of treasure you're putting in your chest. You can choose what kind of story you're telling with your life. As the old saying goes, If you love somebody, set them free. God loves us. So God gives us freedom. God gives us so much freedom that we can go and get ourselves all tangled up in the very things we thought would make us free. Or we can begin to discover the mysterious paradox of God's gracious gift of free will: The more bound we are to God, the freer we are. Imagine how free you will be if you and God are completely one. It encompasses all of life but it starts in the heart.

Our lives conform to a vision. If we are not intentional about setting our vision, the world is perfectly capable of setting one for us. There's a cultural gravity that draws us toward a center, a center mostly of consuming—a center of self. This is the vision we are naturally pulled toward, a default vision of self.

We start sliding that way so we give in to it: envying, buying, loathing, comparing, more buying, doubting, fearing, more envying, more buying, and so on. All these confusing, downward feelings come with the vision that has been given to us. We don't know who we're really supposed to be, so we keep looking around, comparing ourselves to others, buying what we think will make us realize that vision, loathing ourselves when we fail to conform to it, buying something else, doubting our path and fearing we're missing out on something, envying those we think have what we're missing, more buying, moving from false vision to false vision, all spiraling downward toward an empty self, which is empty because it is detached from its true satisfaction found only in God.

Our culture has convinced us that the key to happiness is more—more things, more pleasure, more approval. We attain some thing or some feeling or some achievement, and we experience a little rush. That rush is what we have come to think of as happiness. But the rush wears off. So naturally, we think a little more or a little other is what we need. After all, we're talking about happiness, and who doesn't want more of that! And so, like laboratory mice that keep coming back to feed on crack or sugar until they die, we keep feeding on our inalienable right to the pursuit of happiness. And the cultural gravity continues to pull us.

But instead of pulling us toward the promised happiness, we are pulled toward depression, despair, and ultimately, death. Because the actual result of more and more is the opposite of happiness. Some of us might half-jokingly say that's a chance we're willing to take. But we take that chance every day. And we end up attached. We get attached to the rush and to just a little more—this possession or that relationship or this achievement. Even the *idea* of losing these things makes us depressed, and the *reality* of losing them leads to despair. And this is what our culture calls happiness.

No, the key to happiness is not more. The key to happiness is less. The key to happiness, to fulfillment, to a life worthy of the term, is getting free from attachments and enjoying all of life as it comes . . . and goes.

It is life in the Trinity where we discover our true vision. Sprawling, colorful, electric—the Father, Son, and Spirit are *the* vision, the lens through which we see, as well as the thing that is seen. It plays out differently for each of us, that's how vast it all is—billions of differences . . . it could be trillions and never be exhausted because it's infinite, this Trinity-life. But it is an expansive vision, where a self-centered vision is reductive. Though it is rooted deep within, it moves us outward and grows us, forever.

The difference between self-life and Trinity-life is the difference between bondage and freedom. To live according to that cultural gravity, we have to hold on tight. The cultivation of an image and a lifestyle of means has to be carefully managed, meaning we literally become care-full. We are increasingly concerned about things and about people, though not in a healthy way. We have to put others in their place—either exalted or brought low as the ego dictates—so we can better carve out our own place. The desperation of it all, the grasping at control, has our fists and teeth clinched tight. What's really happening, though, behind the ever-tempting illusion of control, is bondage. Those clenched fists are really bound behind our backs.

The vision of the Trinity is liberation! It liberates us by grace. It is the Father who made us, not the culture, and the Father loves us desperately and knows and wants what is best for us. We learn to trust his love, and this trust is freeing. It is the Son who frees us, not more buying and possessing. He bought us with his own life, so there is no more we can do to get free. Nothing more we can buy, do, imitate, even sacrifice. It is accomplished. And it is the Spirit who guides and empowers us, not the dictates of cultural gravity. The Spirit guides us toward the intimacy and likeness of God, which can't be bought or envied or otherwise attained. It can only be realized in the power of this love working in us. It's there, a vision awaiting discovery, awaiting perfection.

We grow rich, not in goods but in grace. Our prize is the knowledge and love of God. This is both the means and the end. If this isn't enough, then the fault, dear Brutus, is in ourselves. Fellowship fuels fellowship as union fuels union as glory fuels glory . . . and it is the Lord who does this (see 2 Cor. 3:18). Our striving need only be toward God, which is simultaneously a striving toward a greater experience of freedom and a truer vision for our life—a striving toward non-striving.[2] No product, no celebrity, no job or status or relationship or riches of any kind can ever grant us such freedom and meaning and life. All one can do with a vision so glorious is live into it, break free from the pull of cultural gravity and fix ourselves to God's mystery, God's revelation, God's unending embrace. "To all who received him . . . he gave power to become children of God" (John 1:12, NRSV). Here, at this point of receiving him, begins a vision worthy of a child of God. We

---

2. All of this is touching on the apophatic tradition of spirituality, dominant in the Eastern mystic theology of people like Gregory of Nyssa, and bridged to the Western mystic tradition through writers like Pseudo-Dionysius, who wrote, "We leave behind us all our notions of the divine. We call a halt to the activities of our minds and, to the extent that is proper, we approach the ray that transcends being." Pseudo-Dionysius, *Works*, 53. See also the fourteenth century anonymous work *The Cloud of Unknowing*. For a helpful survey of apophatic theology, see Turner, *The Darkness of God*.

have the power to receive him. We have the power to choose this vision. We have the power to will. We have the power to become.

3

It Was Like That When I Got Here

There's a certain spot a few miles outside of my hometown, Canyon, Texas. There are a couple of spots, actually, but they're in the same area. There's a dirt crossroads where friends and I in high school and college used to sit and talk. I don't know how we ended up there—just wandering, I guess. That's how the best spots are usually found. We'd take guitars and harmonicas and sit in the dirt or in the back of someone's pickup and make up blues songs. One July Fourth we went out there late at night and set off fireworks. We had a great time until we got back in Roger's van and discovered the battery was dead. It took several hours to walk the dirt roads back into town and get another car. But we still had fun because we had each other.

Another spot nearby is mostly just mine. There are the remnants of an old, abandoned farmhouse. Cows graze and mill lazily around the cellar door and empty clothesline and rotting barn where a rusted old Ford decays a little more each year. I've spent a lot of time out there alone, under a cloudless blue sky or watching a rose-and-orange sunset or looking up at the black dome thick with stars. I sit on my car or walk the dirt roads. I think and pray. I don't own the land, but since I was young it's been mine.

Just a couple of years ago I learned something that brought a flutter to my gut and tears to my eyes. I was looking at a history of the area and discovered that my ancestors who settled Canyon City (as it was called) back in the late-1800s had, for a time, farmed the exact area where I've spent so many memorable hours. It's such a random place, not easy to get to really. But I've always somehow been drawn to it. And it's the setting for some important parts of my story—parts of my story, as it turns out, that were being told long before I got here.

As I've talked about the heart, I've talked a little about it in terms of the story you're telling with your life. Each of us has a heart, a spiritual will that makes us who we really are and that dictates the direction of our lives. Our story might be about how we pursue money or pleasure or power, about how we climb a ladder to ever-elusive worldly success, about how we try very hard to impress our families and friends and culture. Our story might be about how we are learning to focus our entire lives on walking and working with our Creator, about how we are learning to follow Jesus in the way of God's kingdom. Each of these stories—following the way of creation or following the way of the Creator—does not begin with us. We are merely re-telling or continuing to tell a story that many have told long before us, since the beginning.

As we learn to listen to our hearts, to use our free will to choose the story we tell with our lives, we do well to learn an important truth: God also has a heart. God's heart is, of course, God's will—what God is about, God's goals and God's actions and God's definition of success. You'll remember Samuel, the prophet whom God told that God does not look at the outside like people do, but God looks at our hearts. This Samuel also had some strong words for the wicked king Saul: "You have done a foolish thing . . . You have not kept the command the Lord your God gave you; if you had, he would have established your kingdom over Israel for all time. But now your kingdom will not endure; the Lord has sought out *a man after his own heart*." (1 Sam 13:13–14, my emphasis). Notice how God's heart is so connected to God's commands. The person who follows God's commands, whose will is one with God's will, is a person after God's own heart. If you want to be such a person, if you want your heart to be one with God's heart, then it is vital to come to know God's heart. And who better to reveal the heart of the Father than the Son?

Jesus came on the scene and showed the world myriad things about the Father's heart that we had never before understood. He showed things many people of his time didn't want to understand, things many people today still don't want to understand. The overarching message Jesus brought was what he taught his followers to say to the Father in the intimacy of prayer: "May your kingdom come, may your will be done, on earth as it is in heaven." Jesus's key message was that God's kingdom is coming on earth, coming in and through him and those who follow him. And what is God's kingdom? God's kingdom is God's rule and reign, God's will being done. And what is God's will? In a word, *shalom*.

You might have known the word shalom to mean "peace," and that is correct. But our usual understanding of that peace is drastically insufficient. What shalom really means is universal well-being, peace between God, humanity, and creation that results in abundant life, justice, and flourishing.[1] Shalom is wholeness and, thus, is deeply connected to perfection. This is what we see God willing throughout the Bible. Adam and Eve in the garden, at peace with God and each other and creation. God's covenant with Abraham that the world would be blessed through his many offspring (and through one descendant in particular). The exodus from slavery into the promised "land flowing with milk and honey," and the deliverance and homecoming from exile. In the songs of the psalmists and the visions of the prophets, seeing a new heaven and new earth and a feast on God's holy mountain.[2] Shalom is God's heart. Shalom is God's story.

The story of shalom is most clearly told in Jesus. If you want to know God's heart, look at Jesus. "No one has ever seen God, but the one and only Son, who is himself God and is in closest relationship with the Father, has made him known" (John 1:18). When Jesus heals the sick and provides food for the hungry, he is showing God's heart. When he invites children to come and brings outcasts from the margins to the middle, he is showing God's heart. When he rebukes the hypocrites, recovers the lost, and raises the dead, he is showing God's heart. And when his intimate obedience results in his violent death, and this death exposes evil and frees fallen humanity and creation from their own slavery to sin and death and decay,

---

1. See Holladay, *Lexicon*, 371.

2. God's heart for shalom is articulated in prophetic revelations like God's unfailing "covenant of peace [shalom]" in Isaiah 54:10 and God's "plans for your welfare [shalom]" in Jeremiah 29:11, among many examples. Oswalt notes of Isaiah 54:13 ("great will be the prosperity [shalom] of your children") and its larger context, that the result of covenant relationship with God is shalom. This is not merely a metaphysical union but learning God's ways and replicating God's character. "The disciples of the Lord, the ones filled with his Spirit, are no longer at war with God. They are thus no longer at war with themselves. They are not at war with others: they no longer need to destroy others so that they can aggrandize themselves. They are no longer at war with God's creation; they do not need to carve their initials in it. Such persons have wholeness in themselves, and that wholeness affects all their relationships." Oswalt, *Isaiah*, 428.

and when he is raised to inaugurate the new creation and ascends to rule as king of heaven and earth, he is showing God's heart, God's will for shalom.

And we are meant to join Jesus in all of it—healing and welcoming others, dying to sin and overcoming death, rising again and reigning with God—all of it. God wants us to be set free, to become reborn new creatures, and to live in love and peace with God, with creation, with ourselves, and with our neighbors . . . forever, starting now. And God wants this for the whole world. But how can this ever be?

Jesus was daily confronted with a people whose hearts were moving away from God as they were caught up in telling and re-telling the wrong story. They carried the burden of trying harder and harder to be good enough. They were weighed down with guilt and shame as they climbed a ladder to nowhere, which they were told would lead to success, to perfection. Like oxen yoked together to pull a plow, they were told to be yoked to the Law, which had become a never-ending list of do's and don'ts that only an elite few could ever really hope to understand.

And so, with a heart of mercy and compassion for the poor, enslaved strugglers, Jesus said, "Come to me, all you who are weary and burdened, and I will give you rest. Take my yoke upon you and learn from me, for I am gentle and humble in heart, and you will find rest for your souls. For my yoke is easy and my burden is light" (Matt 11:28–30). How amazing that Jesus, king of heaven and earth, describes his own heart as gentle and humble. No chest thumping and posturing and elbow-throwing power grabs. The way of Jesus, the way of shalom, is the way of the easy yoke and the light burden, of the gentle and humble heart, the way in which those who are weary and burdened can find rest for the deepest parts of their lives.

But it starts with a choice. "Come to me," says Jesus, "all you who are weary and burdened." Come to me. We can't tell two different stories with our lives. If we want to tell the eternal story, the story of God's heart and God's will moving the world toward shalom, then we have to lay down the weight of the worldly story of money and pleasure and power and empty notions of shallow faux-perfection, and step into a new story, yet a story that was being told long before we ever arrived. It's the old story. It's God's story. Come to me.

4

The Plot Thickens

Remember the big secret in *Citizen Kane*? "Rosebud . . . " How about *The Sixth Sense*? Oh, and that crucial revelation in *The Empire Strikes Back*. And the big reveals in *Psycho*, *The Shawshank Redemption*, *The Usual Suspects*, *Fight Club*, *Memento*, *The Sting*. And who knew, in *The Wizard of Oz*, that Dorothy had the power to go home all along? Oh, sorry—spoiler alert! One of the greatest devices a storyteller has for drawing an audience into a story is the plot twist. There are many ways of doing this. But what it always accomplishes is taking what the audience has come to believe is reality and changing it, often profoundly.

Jesus is a master storyteller. And so Jesus often uses plot twists. The rebellious prodigal son comes home. The prodigal's older brother is unhappy about the return of his wayward sibling. Workers who work only one hour get paid the same as those who worked all day. The despised Samaritan is the one who ends up rescuing the favored Jew. A wealthy man dies and ends up in the underworld while a poor beggar dies and goes to the bosom of Abraham. And on and on it goes. The only plot twists that top the ones in Jesus's parables are those in Jesus's real-life actions. "The blind receive sight, the lame walk, those who have leprosy are cleansed, the deaf hear, the dead are raised, and the good news is proclaimed to the poor" (Matt 11:4–5). And the ending, when Jesus is resurrected from the dead and given authority over heaven and earth . . . Oh, sorry—spoiler alert!

In all of this—in Jesus's parables and in Jesus's real life—we see the plot twist, that what the world thought was reality turns out not to be. And instead, reality turns out to be something radically different. We see this, for example, in the beatitudes (Matt 5:1–12). These are often mistaken as a prescription for a good, moral life—do these and you'll be blessed. However, this is not a *pre*scription but a *de*scription. Jesus is describing the new covenant that his followers will find in him, that those who are poor in spirit, hungry for justice, meek, and persecuted are, in fact, *already* blessed.[1] This is a major plot twist because, in their culture, the people Jesus describes (a description that just happened to fit most of his followers) were considered God-forsaken. People would have expected the list to be "blessed are the rich, the powerful, the shrewd and influential—obviously God favors them." Instead, Jesus describes a present and coming kingdom in which the poor and humble and downtrodden not only are lifted up, but turn out to be sons and daughters of the king. Quite a twist!

There is one of those beatitudes that is rather unlike the others. Its promised "payoff" is especially grand. And it just happens to be particularly relevant to our discussion of the heart. "Blessed are the pure in heart, for they will see God." Let's think about that in light of what we've come to understand about the heart. Our heart is our will, what we're about, what drives us, the story we are telling with our lives. We have a free will. We can be driven by things like money, pleasure, and power, telling a story of seeking life apart from the life-giver. Or we can be driven by the desire to be one with this life-giving God, telling a story of God's kingdom coming in the world and in our lives. For as it turns out, God also has a heart, a will, and this is it—this coming peaceable kingdom, described in the word shalom. This shalom is universal well-being, peace among God and humanity and creation that is inextricably connected with things like justice and forgiveness and wholeness of life, individual and collective flourishing.

So, to be "pure in heart" is to be *undivided* in your will. You are not trying to tell two conflicting stories with your life. And, to be pure in heart is to be *unpolluted* in your will. You are not trying to mix the death and darkness of the apart-from-God story with the life and light of God's story. Your story, your will, your heart is *pure*—undivided and unpolluted. Specifically, what this means is that your story is in line with God's story. If God's story is the story of shalom, then you are telling the story of shalom in your own life. You are living every day bringing peace and forgiveness and wholeness into your own life and into the lives and world around you. If characters tell the author's story, they're all on the same page (literally). If characters start telling a different story, as has been the trend in parody books like *Pride and Prejudice and Zombies* and *Sense and Sensibility and*

---

1. Wright explains that the beatitudes are not timeless truths about the way the world is, to be followed for self-improvement, but instead are descriptions of "an upside-down world, or perhaps a right-way-up world . . . It is *gospel*: good news, not good advice." Wright, *Matthew*, 36.

Sea Monsters, the story becomes something quite different from what an author like Jane Austen intended (though she does get a co-author credit in those books—not sure how she'd feel about that).

There are a couple of major differences in the story we're talking about, though. First, we're not talking about fiction but about our real, everyday lives and our real, everyday world. And second, God does not remain merely the author of the world's story. But, in the biggest plot twist in history, God actually writes himself into the story as the main character. Of course God's been the main character all along, but it all becomes clearest in Jesus. "We have seen his glory, the glory of the one and only Son, who came from the Father, full of grace and truth" (John 1:14). So this is the grand fulfillment of the promise: Blessed are the pure in heart, *for they will see God*. If you are telling the divine author's story, this story into which the author has written himself as the main character, then you will come face to face with that author.

So, God is the author and the main character in the world's story, in your story. And we come to learn from this main character, incarnated in time and space as Jesus of Nazareth, of God's profound love for us. But we also learn that the meaning of our lives is to love God "with your whole heart" (Deut 6:5; Mark 12:30). What does this mean? First, love. To love is to will and work for the good of another.[2] If you love your family, then you will and act for the good of your family, even when it costs you something, perhaps even costing your life. You put them first. So, to love God is to will and work for the good of God, even if it costs you something, perhaps even costing your life. You put God first.

Second, the heart. To love God with your heart means to will, from the spiritual core of your being, the good of God.

And third, the whole. To love God with your whole heart is like being "pure in heart." It is to set goals, spend your time, define success, and tell the story of your life according to God's story and God's good.

And what is God's good? Shalom, of course. (You already knew that.) To love God with all your heart, to will and work for the good of God, is to live for peace among God and humanity and creation. Not just a "live and let live" sort of passivity, but an active willing and working toward universal well-being and flourishing among neighbors, nations, and nature, with

---

2. Willard, for example, defines love in terms of *benevolence* ("will to good"), promoting someone or something's good for its own sake. See Willard, *Renovation*, 130.

God at the center . . . at the heart. But be clear, as grand and global as this is, it's *your* story to tell. The story is told in your relationships, your work, your town, your life. It's a story with plot twists that bring a completely new reality into the middle of what everybody thought was real. And—spoiler alert!—the surprise ending is, the story never really ends. It continues to be lived through the purity of your heart as you behold God. It is handed on from generation to generation. And in one more plot twist, as we work with God bringing God's shalom into the world, others come to experience purity of heart, and they begin to see God.

STEPS ON THE JOURNEY

Learning to Love with Your Whole Heart

1. Prayerfully read and consider Jesus's Sermon on the Mount, found in Matthew 5–7. What does this sermon have to do with "loving God with your whole heart" as this section has presented it? Where does the sermon speak of shalom?

2. Do the "elevator pitch" exercise from chapter 1. How would you describe the story your life is telling? In what ways was your life story being told before you were born?

3. In loving God, it is important to honestly share our desires with God. Begin to include in your prayers, "God, I want _____." Consider expressing this in a letter or psalm or poem to God. Let this be the beginning of an ongoing conversation with God about your deepest desires.

4. Where in the world do you see God's shalom? What do you see in the world that works against God's shalom? Now substitute "your life" for "the world."

5. What might it look like for you to love God with your whole heart? Set aside some retreat time (a week, a weekend, a day) to realign your heart with God's heart. (Some helpful resources are Griffin's *Wilderness Time*, Johnson and Lang's *Time Away*, Job and Shawchuck's *Guide to Prayer*, and Warner's *Journey with Jesus*. You might also join a retreat with others and a director.) During your retreat, begin to:

    a. Redefine success for your life. What is really important to you?

    b. Adjust your schedule to allow more time for God—perhaps a slower pace, a lighter schedule, more free time, more efforts toward shalom.

    c. Set realistic, achievable, concrete goals for the next week, month, year, and season of your life that are in line with God's will for your life and for shalom in the world around you.

6. Consider sharing your journey with a spiritual director. This can be especially helpful in keeping one's heart and will in line with God's. There are a number of good resources for finding spiritual directors, including Spiritual Directors International.

PART II

Mind: The Story You Find Yourself In

5

Learning God's Story

Around Halloween, those of us with young children typically have to do some reassuring about the nature of the world we all live in. There aren't ghosts in the attic or monsters in your closet or witches wanting to turn you into a black cat or vampires wanting to suck your blood. It's all in fun, of course, but these ideas can get in kids' heads and really freak them out. We have to help our children learn the true story. We have to reassure them that their home is a safe place, that the world is a safe place. At the same time, we have to warn them about the dangers of the world and the consequences of bad choices. But through it all, it's important for parents to show our children that we love them and we are with them and will take care of them.

Our lives as grownups in the world are no different. Myths, mysteries, and misinformation can get in our heads and affect our thinking. The problem is, as we grow up these wrong ideas result in more than just needing a nightlight. We have a lot more responsibilities and pressures, as well as a lot more influence. More is at stake. But ultimately we want and need the same things as our frightened children—to know that the world is a safe place and that we are loved and taken care of. And God wants nothing less for his children than we want for ours.

This is God's invitation: "Seek the Lord while he may be found; call on him while he is near. Let the wicked forsake their ways and the unrighteous their thoughts. Let them turn to the Lord . . . 'For my thoughts are not your thoughts, neither are your ways my ways,' declares the Lord. 'As the heavens are higher than the earth, so are my ways higher than your ways and my thoughts than your thoughts'" (Isa 55:6–9). Part of the revelation is that God's thoughts and God's ways are higher than ours. But we miss the point when we shrug with a mixture of awe and apathy toward God's transcendence. *God's thoughts and ways are higher than ours*, we think, *so I guess we're on our own.*

The core of this revelation is reached only when we live in the glorious tension of God's transcendence and God's immanence. God is high above us, yet God is intimately present and invites us to come after him. To live the life of faith is to answer Isaiah's prophetic invitation to "seek the Lord" and to "call on him." It is to our deep detriment that we skip this miracle of grace, the miracle that we can "turn to the Lord." You can only really turn to someone who is present. God invites us to seek the Lord and to call on him, to forsake our futility, and instead, to turn to him and journey with him. God has revealed truths about creation, humanity, himself, and his purposes. God wants to help you begin to put these things together so you can have an informed, transformed, beautiful mind. And one of the key ways to form this beautiful mind is to learn God's story. "Seek the Lord while *he may be found*; call on him while *he is near* . . . " This is good news: God is near. God may be found. God's story may be known.

The first part of the story we need to get right in our minds is the nature of creation. The world is not an accident. God made all that is and called it good. Despite what some usually well-meaning folks say and write, the Bible doesn't set out to tell us *how* God made everything. What the Bible tells us is *that* God made everything. Regardless of how it happened, God had a heart for creating and for creation. And God made it for God's glory. God takes great joy and delight in this ongoing project of life and creation. The destiny of the world is not destruction but redemption and glorification. This is something people of faith have gotten terribly wrong, and it bears repeating: The destiny of the world is not destruction but redemption and glorification. This is the work of God and, thus, should be the work of God's people. God is glorified in the very existence of creation, and especially in the wildness and order of the living world as it grows and changes. So our minds need to be shaped by this truth: *The universe and our world are a safe, God-ordained place for us to be.*[1]

The next part of the story we need to understand clearly is the nature of humanity. Just as the world is not an accident, so humans are not accidents. God made humans and called them good. And, like the universe,

---

1. Brueggemann explains that the witness of the Old Testament asserts that "the world is characterized, according to Yahweh's intention and action, as a hospitable, viable place for life, because of Yahweh's will and capacity to evoke and sustain life." Brueggemann, *Theology*, 146.

God made humans for God's own glory. Humans were made in the image of God, more like God in our self-awareness and our capacity to reason and create and love than any other creature in the world. And we were made this way for a special relationship both with God and with creation. We were made to reflect God's glory and will toward creation, and to reflect the glory of creation and the fulfillment of God's will back to God. This is humanity's vocation, our calling. And this is worship.[2]

Of course it's also true that God gives us the freedom to impose our own will in the world. We can choose to work creatively and humbly with God, or to work destructively and pridefully apart from God. Given humanity's special relationship with God and creation, even the existence of natural disasters and diseases is, to some degree, the result of the choice of many to follow the path of destruction, pride, and separation from God. (This is not in any way to say such things are a punishment from God for human sin; only that humanity's unique role among creation is much more deeply and broadly significant and influential than we typically recognize.[3]) And it probably goes without saying that there are plenty of other sins in the world such as theft, abuse, murder, war, greed, exploitation, and on and on, which are the results of wayward humanity. So our minds need to be shaped by this truth: *Humans were made in the image of God to enjoy and glorify God, in large part by helping the world to thrive.*

We've already learned some things about God by learning about the nature of creation and humanity. God is creative. God is joyful and delights in the world and humanity. God is good and wants good things for the world and humanity. God is relational and lives in active relationship with the world and humanity. It's that last one that I want to make sure we get into our thinking, so I might need to restate it more succinctly: *God is present.* God did not set the world in motion and leave. God is with us in the world and even within ourselves. This is what the Bible is mostly about, how God has revealed himself to humanity—especially through this one particular family and people, eventually resulting in God the Son becoming human in a specific time and place as Jesus of Nazareth—and how

---

2. The idea of humans as mirrors (imperfectly) seeing and reflecting God and God's image goes back at least to Paul in, for example, 1 Cor 13:12 and 2 Cor 3:18. See also Augustine, *Trinity*, XV:14, 407–408.

3. Wright, for example, speaks of God's creation project, in which humanity was intended to be God's wise vice-regents bringing order to creation. That project is stalled and incomplete because of humanity's choice to worship creation instead of the Creator. See Wright, "God, 9/11." See also Wright, *Hope*, 94.

humanity has struggled to fulfill its destiny of enjoying and glorifying God and helping the world to thrive. So our minds need to be shaped by this truth: *God is relational and is present in the world and in humanity, drawing us into relationship with himself.*

So what's the point? The final part (for now) of God's story that we need to learn is God's purposes. We've already learned that God's purpose is for humanity to live in right relationship with God and the world, and thus, for all creation to glorify God. But pull back wider, beyond humanity, beyond the world, beyond even the universe or the many universes. Or zoom in closer, closer than your neighborhood or your home or your family or even your own body and soul. Beyond all space and time, and closer than your own life and breath, God is love. God exists in loving relationship within himself—Father, Son, and Holy Spirit—from all time, for all time. Before anything else was, before even space itself was, God is love. And remember that to love is to will and work for the good of the other. So this is God's purpose: love. In the life, death, resurrection, and ascended reign of Jesus, the way is made for us to share in this love. In the abiding presence of the Holy Spirit, we actually live in this love—we inhabit and are inhabited by this love. And as we live in this love, we bring the world into this love. This is God's story. This is the most important truth that needs to shape our minds: *God is love.*

So fill your mind with this story: God made the world in love (willing and working for its good). God made all people in love (willing and working for our good). God loves you (willing and working for your good). God wants you to love (to will and work for the good of God and others). Repeat: God made the world in love. God made all people in love. God loves you. God wants you to love. Repeat . . . If you can think this every day, throughout the day, you will begin to think God's thoughts and to know and follow God's ways. Just because God's thoughts and ways are higher than ours does not mean we can't know them and live them. On the contrary, that's the whole point. Commit yourself to learn God's story. It's time to change your mind.

6

Living God's Story

Nature or grace? That's the question Terrence Malick's beautiful film *The Tree of Life* poses, presenting life as a choice between the path of nature or the path of grace. In the film, Malick tackles nothing less than the creation of the world. At one point there is a scene featuring a sick, weakened dinosaur lying in a shallow creek. Another dinosaur spots the sick one and rushes over. It steps on the weak one's head and is prepared to destroy it. After a moment, the strong one appears to change its mind. It thoughtfully removes its foot from the other's head and finally runs off. Malick seems to be showing this as a very early example of compassion, of choosing the path of grace over the path of nature.

Most of the rest of the movie unfolds around a family in 1950s Texas. The father lives a life of frustration and struggle, in part the result of his choice to give up his dreams of being a musician in order to earn a living for his family as an engineer. He is very stern and demanding of his three sons, struggling to reconcile his love for them with what he feels is his responsibility to toughen them up for life in the harsh world. He represents the path of nature. The mother, on the other hand, is gentle and nurturing, though no less an authority in the boys' lives. Her care offers her sons freedom in a worldview that sees the world not as fearful, but wonderful. She represents the path of grace.

The path of nature or the path of grace. We could make it more specific and say life centers largely on a choice between following a gracious God or attempting to live apart from such a God, apart from grace. The question is addressed in terms of philosophies and worldviews including ideas like rationalism, empiricism, humanism, and even materialism and atheism, as opposed to the theism and spirituality we see in Christianity. Is the world as we encounter it all there is? And so, is life as we experience it through our senses and observable phenomena all there is? Or is there more, something above and beyond it all, yet perhaps intimately close? Is there a "higher purpose" as we often say when we speak of God and God's plans? We see this choice in world history and in current events. We make this choice in our minds—and live it in our lives—on a daily basis, especially in the way we think about the essence or fundamental character of creation, humanity, God, and God's purposes.

As we've already come to understand, the first key to forming a godly mind is learning God's story. Of course, what we're calling God's story is really only the tip of an unfathomably deep and vast iceberg. But often the best way to approach God's vastness and incomprehensibility is through simplicity. So, we've begun to approach God's story in this practicable way:

- The essence of creation: God made the world in love.
- The essence of humanity: God made all people in love.
- The essence of God: God is love and God loves you.
- The essence of God's purposes: God wants you to love.

The second key to forming a godly mind, then, would be *living* God's story. Like those lists of rules that say things like "Rule #2: Learn Rule #1," this is indeed the case with living God's story. In order to live God's story, we must continue to learn God's story. The fundamentals we discussed in the previous chapter are only a very rough starting place. The only way to truly learn God's story is to live God's story, and *vice versa*. But continuing to learn God's story would be the path of grace. The flip side of the same coin would be to learn the so-called path of nature, the path apart from the gracious God (in the way I'm presently using "nature"). By this I mean learn to recognize where the world's story deviates from God's story. Both are vital. This is how we live our lives as part of God's story, how we come to truly and faithfully play our role in this grand narrative. And it starts in our thinking. So, regarding the essence of creation, humanity, God, and God's purposes, following are some thoughts on the path of nature (life apart from God) versus the path of grace (life with God) and, specifically, the choice to follow a gracious God or not. Each point is concluded (in good, logical fashion) with an "if/then" statement about living God's story.

Regarding Creation: *Nature* says the world is to be dominated and consumed. This is rooted in the idea that the world is a godless and fearful place. This results in a disconnect from nature and nature's good, as well as from God and God's plans. The emphasis is on taking.

Grace says God made the world in love. The Bible teaches that God intentionally created the world as a safe place, and God inhabits the world with his creatures. The emphasis is on God's giving. So, *if* God made the world in love and inhabits it with his creatures, *then* I need to invest my life in helping the world to thrive. Learning to see the world as full of God's glory, and setting your mind on how you, in your specific context, can help the world to thrive, is living God's story.

Regarding Humanity: *Nature* says only the strongest survive, and this is as it should be for the propagation of desirable traits and, thus, the achievement of success in the world. (Despite similar language, I am not attempting to speak of evolution, anthropology, etc., but of generally accepted cultural practices and of the choice between embracing or shunning God's grace.) This "survival of the fittest" mentality is rooted in the fear that people will hurt me, whether physically or emotionally, and it includes the fear that I might fail or be negatively judged. I must thus cultivate and project strength and dominance, even at the expense of others. This results in comparison (feeling superior or inferior), inauthenticity (projecting a false image), and segregation (shutting out people who are different and/or who threaten my sense of superiority). The emphasis is on gaining and wielding power.

Grace says God made all people in love. The Bible teaches that God made all people—*all* people—in God's image to enjoy and glorify God on earth. The emphasis is on serving. So, *if* God made all people in love, *then* I need to help people to thrive. Learning to see others as made and loved by God, and setting your mind on how you can help them to thrive, is living God's story.

Regarding God: *Nature* says God is superstition, distant, or angry. This is rooted in the human desire to control, especially to control other humans and the unknown, and to do so by propagating notions of god after humanity's own image. It results in fragmentation (if God is superstition, then there is no ultimate, integrating meaning), fear (if God is distant, then the world is godforsaken and there is no tangible hope), and shame (if God is angry, then any attempt to relate to God must be grounded in humiliation and alienation). The emphasis is on human and personal autonomy.

Grace says God is love and God loves me. The Bible teaches that not only *does* God love, but God *is* love. And God is present in the world and within humanity, drawing all into loving relationship with himself. The emphasis is on union with God. So, *if* God is love and God loves me, *then* I need to consider God and myself objects of love. Learning to see yourself as connected to God, and setting your mind on how you can open yourself to receive and return God's love, is living God's story.

Regarding God's Purposes: *Nature* says, "Let us eat and drink, for tomorrow we die."[1] This is rooted in the fear of death. It results in self-centeredness and materialism, especially life consumed with the pursuit of material wealth, pleasure, and power. Included in this are all manner of ways to numb oneself to the sense of life's futility and pain, whether through substance abuse, illicit or harmful sexual practices, overwork, overeating, reckless and self-centered attempts to make one's mark in the world, and so on. The emphasis is on self and escape.

Grace says the God who is love wants us to love. The Bible teaches that God, in God's relentless love, has conquered death and invites us to share in God's eternal life and love, life and love with God in the world today and in eternity forever. The emphasis is on being present (in the moment and to others). So, *if* God loves all and wants me to love, *then* I need to consider others worthy of love. Learning to see beyond yourself, and setting your mind on sharing God's love with others, is living God's story.

Picking up from Isaiah's invitation (discussed in the previous chapter) to seek and call on the Lord so that we might know God and learn God's higher ways (Isa 55:6–9), God continues speaking through the prophet with words on living these ways:

> As the rain and the snow come down from heaven, and do not return to it without watering the earth and making it bud and flourish, so that it yields seed for the sower and bread for the eater, so is my word that goes out from my mouth: It will not return to me empty, but will accomplish what I desire and achieve the purpose for which I sent it. You will go out in joy and be led forth in peace; the mountains and hills will burst into song before you, and all the trees of the field will clap their hands. Instead of the thornbush will grow the juniper, and instead of briers the myrtle will grow. This

---

1. 1 Corinthians 15:32. Appropriate for our discussion of a godly mind, Paul follows this example of the despair of death without the hope of resurrection with the teaching, "Come to a sober and right mind, and sin no more, for some people have no knowledge of God . . ." (verse 34).

will be for the LORD's renown, for an everlasting sign, that will endure forever (verses 10–13).

This is about the life-giving revelation of God that overcomes the curse of Genesis 3. This is all about God's shalom, the peace and flourishing between God and humans and creation. Read the passage again and notice how interconnected it all is: God lavishes his grace on creation and humanity in the form of rain that nourishes nature, which in turn yields seed for grain and bread to nourish humans. This cycle is an illustration of God's revelatory word and revealed will that nourish humanity and creation by accomplishing God's purposes, which again are illustrated by the flourishing of nature. And all of this glorifies God and will endure forever. This is God's story, to be learned and to be lived. So, some principles for *living* God's story might be:

- Make yourself at home in the world. (God is here.)
- Make others at home in the world. (Join God in welcoming all.)
- Trust God's goodness. (God loves you and wills and works for your good.)
- Share God's goodness. (Join God in willing and working for the good of all.)

This way of living is a way of participating in God's grace and God's story. In this way we become like the heavenly rain, bearers of God's living, nourishing word and loving revelation transforming the world.

7

Learning Your Story

Imagine your favorite story. It could be a book, a movie, a play, a TV show, even a song. For the sake of discussion, let's choose *The Wizard of Oz*. Now imagine that you don't know the setting. We know it's Kansas and Oz. But what if you didn't know. Is it eighteenth-century France? Is it 1970s New York City? Is it a distant galaxy a thousand years in the future? And what about the main character, Dorothy; what's she like? Is she a good witch or a bad witch? Or is she an evil man disguised as a precocious teenaged girl? And what's the driving force behind this story? Is Dorothy trying to catch the man who killed her father? Is the scarecrow trying to find his lost love? And what kind of story is this, anyway? Is it a gun-down-the-bad-guy western? Is it a courtroom drama? Are the Munchkins zombies?

There are a couple of ways to find out the nature of the story. We can research and investigate the setting, the lead character, the story's driving force, and its genre. Or we can let the story speak for itself. But either way, or with some combination of both, if we don't understand some key things about the nature of the story, things get very confusing. If you actually watch *The Wizard of Oz*, thinking the entire time that this is a movie about a man disguised as a girl who's trying to avenge the death of his father while living in 1970s New York City . . . and being chased by Munchkin zombies . . . things are not going to make much sense (though it might be awesome!). Something has to change.

Your story is no different. Your life is telling a story every day. Most of it is unremarkable, which is usually a good thing. Occasionally, big things happen—good and bad. Something big happened when you started intentionally joining your story to God's story: a new story began to emerge. If you aren't intentional about understanding the setting of your story, the chief characteristic of your lead character, the driving force of your story, and what kind of story you're telling, things get very confusing. In fact, most of us don't understand these things and, thus, live in a nearly constant state of confusion. So, in the name of cultivating a godly and beautiful mind, you must begin to learn your story.

The setting of your story is God's kingdom. Many make one of two mistakes regarding the kingdom of God. On the one hand, they relegate God's kingdom to a footnote in Jesus's ministry. There is some understanding of God's kingdom as having some positive effect in the world, but it's just the result of Christians being nice. Jesus really only came to get us into heaven when we die. Any apparent connection of the kingdom of God with "social justice" issues was a byproduct of Jesus's soft spot for the little guy, but was not of eternal significance or great importance to Jesus's ministry.

On the other hand, the more common mistake is to change the meaning of the kingdom of God altogether, relegating it to an after-life in heaven. This is, to some degree, an honest mistake based in part on the Gospel of Matthew's frequent use of the expression "the kingdom of heaven," which he possibly used instead of "kingdom of God" simply as a reverential attempt to avoid using the word "God," and especially to illustrate the supreme nature and heavenly origin of that kingdom. However, Matthew's wording is not to indicate the *place* of this rule but the *nature* of this rule. It isn't referring only to the reign of God we will experience when we've died and gone to heaven. It means the reign of God in God's special "domain" having its way in this world, typically understood as only the domain of humans and human rulers. So, when Jesus says, "Repent, for the kingdom of heaven has come near" (Matt 4:17), what he is saying is something like, "Change your thinking and your life's direction and realign your allegiances, for the heavenly rule of God has come to earth!" These are words of revolution. And far from a footnote, this is what Jesus was about as much as, or more than, anything else.

This revolutionary kingdom is the landscape of your story. And what does this mean? What characterizes this kingdom? Is it about a group of elites parsing out a list of do's and don'ts, a "Gotcha!" club standing in judgment against the increasing number of outsiders? Quite the contrary. "Therefore let us stop passing judgment on one another . . . For the kingdom of God is not a matter of eating and drinking, but of righteousness, peace and joy in the Holy Spirit" (Rom 14:13, 17). So, from the outset we understand that your story—and, for our present purposes, your mental landscape—is characterized by:

- Righteousness, by which is meant justice with peace and freedom, the repentance and realigned allegiances of Jesus's call, and the commitment to follow God's will for God's glory;
- Peace, which is the shalom we discussed previously, the universal well-being and wholeness with God, neighbor, self, and creation;
- Joy, an abiding delight and sense of contentment in God's intentional creation and constant care, experienced as a result of the powerful indwelling of God the Holy Spirit.

So, the setting in which your story unfolds is God's kingdom, including a mental landscape (resulting in an outward life) of righteousness, peace, and joy in the Holy Spirit.

And now, about the lead character: you. (I wrote previously about God being the main character. But for our present purposes, we're thinking less in terms of the grand universal story and more in terms of the story you are telling with your own free life, especially joined with God's.) You might think of yourself in terms of physical characteristics, abilities, family, work, and so on. But the main characteristic of you, your story's lead character, is the image of God. The creation story in Genesis explains how God created humankind—male and female—in God's own image, telling us to be fruitful and increase in number, to fill the earth and govern it, and to have dominion over every living thing (see Gen 1:27–28).

Misunderstandings about, and abuse of, this role and relationship to God and creation have abounded. We have thought being made in God's image was tantamount to being God. We have thought the expression "be fruitful and multiply" simply meant to have children, at times even considering it a duty with no regard for love or mutual consent. And perhaps most notoriously, we have thought subduing the earth and having dominion was license for global ecological destruction and death in the name of human superiority. We even used such thinking to justify other evils like slavery, for example, reducing Africans to a sub-human status and enslaving them in the name of exercising dominion over creatures. Thinking such abuses were the most expedient and cost-effective path to human flourishing, instead we were setting our own house on fire in the name of building a better mousetrap. And akin to mistaking the kingdom of God for only the afterlife in heaven, many Christians have historically supported horrendous environmental abuses because they believe they'll "fly away" from it all and leave the earth to a divine destiny of destruction. But nothing could be further from the truth, or further from what it means for us to be made in God's image.

So what does it mean that you, your story's main character, are made in and live in God's image, and what's more, that this is your defining characteristic? First, we must consider the idea of image. You live in a special position between God and creation. As a human, you are uniquely able to reflect the glory and will of God toward creation. You can know God in a special way. You can at least begin to understand God's character and purposes, and to choose to live in deepening intimacy with God. So, you are uniquely positioned to live out God's shalom, to bring righteousness, peace, and joy to bear in the world, especially as part of the joyous life of the Father, Son, and Holy Spirit. You reflect the glory of God into the world.

Also within the idea of image, you are a part of creation uniquely positioned to reflect the glory of creation back to God. All creation glorifies God in its own way, from the vast mystery and majesty of mountains and oceans, to the equally majestic and mysterious complexity of DNA and quarks. But humans like you are able to recognize, explore, harness, and articulate the majesty and mystery of creation as the glorious product of its Creator. This is a life posture that embraces all of life as worship. You creatively and intentionally reflect the glory of the world back to God.

Next is fruitfulness. You are called to "be fruitful and multiply." It is a joy and a blessing to make more humans and, especially, to raise them in the way of shalom. Indeed, such fruitfulness and multiplication is an essential component of shalom. But this is not merely the idea of *procreation*. This calling is also very much about *co*-creation. You have the gift of creativity. You may or may not consider yourself a creative person. But as one made in God's image, you are made for fruitful creativity. Whether you are a teacher, mechanic, attorney, farmer, stay-at-home mom or dad, doctor, engineer, service-member, musician, social worker, restaurant server, artist, businessperson, retail worker, pastor, scientist, poet, first responder, or you are following just about any vocation or healthy way of spending a life, you are part of God's work of creation. You are helping to make this world what it is, ideally in positive and even godly ways.

Your life and work may seem unglamorous to you, perhaps even insignificant. But I assure you God doesn't see it that way. The simplest, humblest life is as much a part of God's creative power and will in the world as is the grandest, most striking life. Your life is something that has never been before, nor will it be again. Your very existence is an expression of divine creativity. Understand what I am *not* saying. I am not saying your life is about *doing* a bunch of grand, important things. I am saying the fruitfulness you are made for is the natural result of *becoming* the person God intends you to be. And that is more likely to happen by letting go of the ego's need to be important and, instead, resting in your importance as one beloved of God. Your life of fruitfully reflecting God's glory to creation and creation's glory to God is part of your main characteristic as bearing God's image.

Finally, there's dominion. You are made with reason and a unique ability to order your life and the world immediately around you. You are an agent of God's shalom, not merely able, but divinely called to employ your life in helping the world and others toward wholeness and flourishing. No matter your resources, abilities, and connections, or lack thereof, you are made to exercise dominion in the world. Your dominion might be in a classroom, in a small business or large corporation, in a family, in government, in the arts, in a neighborhood, or in any number of spheres of influence. Your dominion certainly includes your life and the way you interact with other lives. For some, their dominion was in the horror of a concentration camp. For others, it was as slave labor in a cotton field. For many, their dominion has been a battlefield, whether a physical battlefield, emotional battlefield, spiritual battlefield, or some combination.

Many people—especially in situations like these—have felt they have no dominion whatsoever. But whether one is in an operating room as doctor or patient, or in a prison as guard or prisoner, we all have dominion. We have dominion of mind, of spirit, of faith and hope and love. We have this dominion because we have the divine image. You are, thus, divinely made, gifted, and appointed to help order the world within you and around you, to help bring God's kingdom on earth as it is in heaven. You are made to join your life to creation and to other lives—even just one other life—and to lovingly serve them so that they may more perfectly reflect and glorify the goodness and good will of the one who made them.

So God's image is your chief characteristic, the foundation of the character through whom your story is told. Image, fruitfulness, and dominion. Reflection, creativity, and order. Perhaps this doesn't sound like you. Maybe you think of yourself more in terms like cloudy, infertile, and chaotic. And maybe you've experienced life in ways that give you good reason to think of yourself in terms that are anything *but* the image of God. But if I can relate anything at this point it would be this: You have a choice. Making this choice can be difficult, and living it can be far more so. But you can let others define you—perhaps as who you used to be or who they want you to be, as a misguided lead character or even an insignificant bit player in your own life. Or you can accept the reality of your identity on God's terms, that you are a chip-off-the-ol'-block child of your heavenly Father, who made you a bearer of his glory and a teller of his story. Made in the image of the God who is Love, you too are love.

So what drives this story? Certainly the setting (God's kingdom) and the main character's main characteristic (God's image) give significant impetus. But what is the plot, the main theme, the big idea that keeps this story moving forward? A key to a compelling story is that the main character must be trying to attain some thing, some place, and/or some state of being. So what is it you're after? What *should* you be after? Are they the same? What drives you to get out of bed day after day, year after year? Perhaps it's just the routine. But you were born for more than paying bills and dying—far more. The driving force of your story is union with God. It's quite possible that you thought the driving force of your story was success, making a difference in the world, being a good person, or even "getting saved." Each of those things (and many more) is a result of, and related to, union with God. But they are not the main thing. To understand this main thing we must listen to some dying words.

There are many stories of deathbed wisdom and end-of-life clarity, the perspective that comes from knowing the end is near and the final words that often accompany that lofty view from the mountaintop. The writers of the four Gospels devote half of their respective books to the last week of Jesus's life, in which Jesus utters much of his characteristic divine wisdom and clarity of vision. John, for example, devotes four chapters (14-17) to some of the most profound and moving words of Jesus's teaching, all apparently taking place after the last supper on the Thursday night on which Jesus is later arrested. The next day he is crucified. So this is essentially Jesus's final discourse, his last words shared with his closest friends and followers who will go on to start and be the church and share Jesus's teaching with the world. They will share Jesus's teaching especially by embodying it. And most of them will, like their master, be killed as a result. So, needless to say, Jesus is really getting to the heart of things at this point. If they've learned nothing else in all these months of sharing life with him, this is the essential thing. This is the driving force of his mission, of his story, and thus of all who will share in it. And what is it? Union—that we would be one. Union with God. And union with each other *in* God. There are many details, metaphors, and different ways Jesus uses to get at his point. But *that* is his point through all four of these chapters: Become one with the Father, Son, and Holy Spirit, and with each other.

Here's the thing about union with God, a fact most of us spend our entire lives missing: You and God are already united. Before you were born you were an idea in the mind of God, and, thus, you were one with God.[1] Your very existence is the result of union with God. Just as it was with the first *adam* (human), the "breath" of God is what gives us life. God's breath isn't air, as we think of breath. But the same way air-breath helps deliver life-giving oxygen into our bodies, so God's breath delivers the essence of life to all living things. In the words of a poet, "All creatures look to you . . . When you hide your face, they are terrified; when you take away their breath they die and return to the dust. When you send your Spirit, they are created, and you renew the face of the ground" (Ps 104:27, 29–30). If you were not one with God you would cease to exist. You are here on purpose. God knows you. God made you. Regardless of your thoughts about biology, human conception, evolution, or any "back story" information on how you got here, the fact remains: You only exist because God wants you to exist. God is responsible for every nanosecond of your aliveness, your being. Thus, your life of faith is merely a collaboration with God on what God has been doing the entire time. Waking up to this reality is a major step in learning your story.

But here's the other thing about union with God: You have to discover it. That's why union with God is the driving force of your story, the thing you're after. You have to pursue it for the rest of your life, by which I mean forever. It's like the classic plot twist where the hero had what she needed inside herself . . . , or the treasure was right under his nose . . . , or they had been in the place they were looking for . . . the whole time! So it is with union with God. We are already united with God, yet pursuit of that union is the point of all our striving, the ultimate treasure, the end of our journey

---

1. This is connected to the concept of exemplarism, adapted and developed from Plato and Plotinus by Augustine, Aquinas, Bonaventure, and others. It is rooted in Christ as our exemplar and the Son and true Image of God.

(which turns out to be another beginning). But we must go on the journey nonetheless. Only then can we begin to truly see, to truly know, where and who we truly are.

It is a city within us, buried under years of struggle and pain and distractions and sin. And so we must excavate. It is maturity within us, still distant with years of struggle and pain and discipline and nurture. And so we must grow. It is the oak within the acorn. "Dear friends, now we are children of God, and what we will be has not yet been made known. But we know that when Christ appears, we shall be like him, for we shall see him as he is" (1 John 3:2–3).

This is the driving force of your story, to "be like him." This does not refer merely to outward behavior. Jesus's holy behavior emerged in large part from his union with the Father in the love of the Holy Spirit—it was not only what he did but who he was. And he commends the same to us. He prayed to the Father in his final hours, "I have given them the glory that you gave me, that they may be one as we are one—I in them and you in me—so that they may be brought to complete unity. Then the world will know that you sent me and have loved them even as you have loved me" (John 17:22–23). Complete unity. Perfection in love.

So the driving force of your story is to uncover the union with God that lies within you . . . and yet, in so many ways, beyond you. This is the thing for which you will struggle both outwardly and inwardly, even as it lives in your own soul. The setting of your story is God's kingdom—you're in it (and more to the point, it is in you) yet somehow still so far from it. The main characteristic of you as your story's main character is God's image—you're made in it, yet the likeness is still fuzzy in so many ways. And the driving force of your story is attaining union with God—you're already one, yet there's still so much distance between you. And so you press on to take hold of that for which Christ Jesus took hold of you (see Phil 3:12). You've already been taken hold of, yet you must press on to take hold of the one who is already holding you. How simultaneously fascinating and frustrating it all is.

Before we continue, let me caution you against a mistake made by many over the centuries who have told this same story. You are not God. You never will be God. This may already be painfully apparent to you (or certainly to those around you). But the temptation to fall into this heresy is a last bastion of dangerous waywardness for many whose stories are driven by this same union seeking. After all your uncovering and discovering and finding yourself more and more able to "participate in the divine nature" (2 Pet 1:4), it can become (for some at least) increasingly tempting to withdraw from Christian community and loving correction and growth in grace, to believe oneself independently divine and even to have in some way become the God one was seeking. But no matter how close to God you become, no matter how united in love and knowledge even to the extent of no longer seeing much difference, the difference remains. It's like pointing a flashlight (you) at the sun (God): No matter how united and brilliant the light, your light is still your light and God's light is still God's light—you are still you and God is still God.

Yet this union is the thing you were made for. You were made to participate in the life of the Trinity. But it is only through participating in the saving work of Jesus Christ the Son of God, through the power of the Holy Spirit, to the glory of God the Father that you are enabled to tell this story. Nevertheless, this is your story to tell. This is what drives it. At the end of it all (though again, it never really ends), you can look back at your life of faith and say, "This is the story of how I became one with God." It sounds rather like a love story, don't you think?

And so we arrive at the genre of your story. This in many ways seems like the simplest aspect, yet it can also be the most confusing. What kind of story is this complicated series of moments and days and seasons? It's a mystery. It's a tragedy. It's a comedy. It's a mixture of non-fiction and fiction rolled into an autobiography. It's even a fantasy with monsters and heroes on epic quests, and science fiction (and fact) as you search for meaning among astounding life forms and technologies on a terrestrial ball hurtling through the dark and brilliant expanse of space. But none of these is the true genre of your story, though it's easy to get bogged down in one of these characteristics and lose the big picture. Yet in Jesus the big picture and genre have been made clear: It's a love story.

Your life may or may not contain romance and affection. You might or might not have experienced the doting love of parents and family, the loving camaraderie of friends. And while such experiences can go far in helping us appreciate the nature of our story as a love story, in the end they are not so essential to the fact. For no lover, parent, or friend has the power to determine the nature of your story. It has already been set and is only for you to live it out. It is a love story . . . an epic love story.

In that final discourse, Jesus spells it out quite clearly. "As the Father has loved me, so have I loved you. Now remain in my love. If you keep my commands, you will remain in my love, just as I have kept my Father's commands and remain in his love. I have told you this so that my joy may be in you and that your joy may be complete. My command is this: Love each other as I have loved you" (John 15:9–12). That's seven "loves" in four verses. I think Jesus has a point to make here. He is giving us our love story and setting out three "states of love," if you will, through which we are to tell that story.

The first state is *receiving* love. "As the Father has loved me, so have I loved you." Imagine the relentless ferocity of that love! As the Father has loved the Son, that's the kind of love Jesus the Son has for his followers. This is eternal love, divine love that is shaped by existing from all time and for all time. This love lays down its life for the good of the beloved. And the beloved is you, the church, and the world (see John 3:16). But have you received that love? The question isn't merely do you *believe* in that love. The question is have you *received* it? Do you regularly receive it? Does it wash over and through you, shaping you and moving you and transforming you into its own likeness? Have you let it rescue you? Seriously. I said this is an epic love story. And anyone who knows anything about epic love stories knows that at some point the beloved is held captive and must be set free. So, have you been liberated by this love, freed from the clutches of hopelessness and bitterness and emptiness and desperation, and filled with the bread and wine of life-giving love?

Many people live years attempting to follow Jesus and never awaken to this first state of receiving his love. They carry shame and guilt like shackles on their heart and mind. They think themselves unworthy to participate in this grand love story, sure that if anyone—and especially Jesus—knew who they really were inside, there would be no love for them. So why bother? The tragedy is that they are severely underestimating the power of this love. "As the Father has loved me . . . " That's the kind of love Jesus has for them, for you, for all. There aren't words for this kind of love. It can't be explained. It is told throughout the scriptures, through the narratives of Jesus's life and death and conquering of death and ascended reign—all of which are driven by this love. Yet even these stories can't really convey what actually receiving this love into one's life conveys. So I'll leave it there. No words. Just the life-transforming experience of receiving this love.

The second state is *living in* this love. "If you keep my commands, you will remain in my love, just as I have kept my Father's commands and remain in his love." This is the daily grind of love—the messy stuff. This is the point at which so many people in the world say they "fell out of love" with their significant other. In actuality it was a choice not to remain in love. Occasionally it is warranted. More often it is disenchantment with the work love takes. The word for "remain" carries the idea of relationship to a state of being, which is my point here. Jesus tells us to continue relating to the state of loving and being loved. But I also like the translations that have Jesus saying, ". . . abide in my love" (NRSV). To abide is to live or dwell in something. So the image is that this is the kind of love you move in to. This love is your dwelling place, your home.

This is why Jesus explains it in terms of keeping his commands. Abiding and remaining in love through the tough times requires discipline. It takes commitment. You don't move out of your house when the roof leaks. You remain in it and work on it. So much of love is about showing up. And that's what Jesus is saying: Keep showing up. Keep working alongside Jesus, learning and practicing his way of grace and mercy and forgiveness and obedience. Obedience, because Jesus doesn't ask anything of us that he hasn't demonstrated himself—"just as I have kept my Father's commands and remain in his love." Again we are brought into the life-giving, transformational love of the Father and Son as our example and source. No matter how challenging Jesus's circumstances got, how tempted he might have been to follow a different path, he chose to stay obedient to the Father and to remain in his love. And we know it got messy for Jesus. But we also see how the Father's love was Jesus's shelter from the storm. The good news is that Jesus continues to get messy loving us right where we are every day. He built the house. It is up to us to move in and live there.

The third state is *sharing* this love. "My command is this: Love each other as I have loved you." Most Christians think they have a pretty good handle on this one. We try to get along with people, to not do bad things, and even to do some good in the world. The problem is, we try to live in this last state without living in the first two. We try to love others without really receiving and remaining in Christ's love. So when he says to love others "as I have loved you," we really have no idea what that means, no idea how Jesus loves. He told us to look at the love he shares with the Father. That is our model. If we don't have that, then we settle for whatever approximation of love we can cobble together. "As I have loved you"—that's a really important part of the equation. It's like how the flight attendant tells parents with small children to put on their own oxygen mask first. It's kind of hard to help others when you're blacked out and slumped over in your seat. Receiving and living in Christ's love is like an oxygen mask for your soul, through which the Holy Spirit breathes life-giving love into your being.

And this enables you to love others . . . as he has loved you. In many ways it becomes easier at that point, or at least much more natural. When you are in the states of receiving and remaining in Christ's love, it's all but impossible not to share it. Your story truly becomes a love story, your mind transformed in the exalted adoration of Father, Son, and Spirit. You see opportunities to love. You feel the need for love around you. You are attuned to the harmony and discord of the lives you encounter every day. And now you know how to love them. You have love to share. You are now part of the river of God's love that is always flowing toward all people and creation. You move with God's love as it flows to you, around you, and from you—receiving, remaining, and sharing. And so begins the love story of your life. What it looks like will be unique for you. But one thing is sure, it will be epic!

The result of entering into this love story is that we come full circle, back to our earlier discussion of your story's setting in God's kingdom. "I have told you [to receive, remain in, and share my love] so that my joy may be in you and that your joy may be complete." We learned that God's kingdom is characterized by "righteousness, peace and joy in the Holy Spirit" (Rom 14:17). This joy is not simply happiness (for which it is often mistaken). True joy is God-derived and God-focused. This joy is a sense of delight and contentment in the world and in ourselves because we recognize that God is present in both.

In his book *The Return of the Prodigal Son*, Henri Nouwen makes a crucial observation about Jesus's parables in Luke 15, featuring a shepherd looking for his lost sheep, a woman looking for her lost coin, and a father eagerly awaiting the return of his lost son—each of whom represents God. Nouwen writes, "God rejoices. Not because the problems of the world have been solved, not because all human pain and suffering have come to an end, nor because thousands of people have been converted and are now praising him for his goodness. No, God rejoices because *one* of his children who was lost has been found. What I am called to is to enter into that joy."[2]

---

2. Nouwen, *Return*, 114.

We miss that joy, says Nouwen, because it is small, hidden, and inconspicuous. The temptation is constant (and has only gotten stronger since Nouwen wrote this in the 1990s) to find joy only in the grand, impressive, and showy. Even in matters of faith, it is easy to see God and find joy only in big, miraculous gestures of healing, conversion, worship, and the like. But the nature of joy I've come to understand would say otherwise. "You show me the path of life. In your presence there is fullness of joy; in your right hand are pleasures forevermore" (Ps 16:11, NRSV). It is God's presence that brings joy, not the presence of any dazzling spectacle. Sure, the spectacular might point to God's presence. But so can the unspectacular, the quiet, the simple—sometimes even more so, for those who have eyes to see and ears to hear. And that's what it comes to: attentiveness.

If joy depends on rejoicing in God's presence—in the everyday as much as in the once-in-a-lifetime—then we must learn to recognize God's presence. Where might God be working in a life, in the world, in creation, in an "average" day, in the deep quiet of your own soul? May we find ourselves ever more in the habit of pausing to observe and to rejoice in moments of small, hidden, quiet joy . . . each of which, for God, is likely cause for a party.

That joy, beloved one, is the source and result of a beautiful, godly mind. And that mind is the source and result of fully participating in your story, which depends greatly on learning your story. All the thoughts and feelings you have—the demons of the past, the distractions of the present, and the doubts about the future—are all filtered through the reality of joy. You experience delight and contentment in the world and in yourself because you are learning to recognize that God is powerfully and lovingly present in both. Your mind is running out of room for the death-dealing unhealthy thoughts and feelings about the world, about your neighbor, and about yourself, because your mind is filled with Christ's joy. This joy born of love is becoming complete in us, says Jesus. This completion is closely aligned to the idea of perfection—not finished, but also not lacking. Joy is a big part of what happens to your mind as you learn your story:

- You live in God's kingdom. Nothing can destroy it. The setting of your story includes, of course, many other aspects. And it is vital to come to understand and relate to the space in which you live—its history, its people, its daily routines and seasonal rhythms. God made that place and is active there. In fact, God's activity continues to make that place, and you are invited to be involved in forming your own setting. This, though, is simply more of what is meant by God's kingdom come on earth.

- You bear God's image. God is love and so are you. You have many other characteristics to your life—some good, some otherwise. It is vital to come to know all aspects of your life, the good and bad. God is at work in all parts of you, to conform you more to God's likeness so you might more fully experience God's love moving into and out of you. This work, painful as it sometimes is, is simply part of bearing God's image.

- You are one with God. Nothing can separate you from God. There may be many things that drive you, many goals you hope to achieve and a grand journey you are on that is unlike that of anyone else. This is all wonderful! But again, your unique journey and goals are simply part of your experience of simultaneously living in and moving toward union with God.

- You are made for love. God loves and so can you. You are telling many kinds of stories in your life. And life itself may not seem like much of any kind of story at all, especially while it's happening. And more, life may not seem remotely like a *love* story. But this is based on a deficient cultural understanding of love. The very fact of your existence is the result of love. It might or might not be the result of love between your parents. But it is certainly the result of God's love. You were born of and for love.

So this is your story's basic framework within which your unique life is lived. Setting: *God's kingdom*. Character: *God's image*. Plot: *Union*. Genre: *Love*. If I may, I'd like to offer a sort of daily affirmation. I pray it often, especially when I'm feeling stressed, fearful, depressed, anxious, or just generally mentally discombobulated. It's simply a summary of our shared story—yours, mine, and God's—and I commend it to you. It goes like this: "I live in your kingdom. I live in your image. We are one. We are love." Resting into God's presence, I repeat that affirmation as often as necessary until my mind has focused on the truth of my story rather than the misinformation—the choking mental weeds—constantly coming from my culture, my past, my anticipated future, and my wayward mind. I have to say there are moments, maybe more often than not, that I come to a point where I feel God affirming me as I affirm this story. And I begin to think differently.

8

Living Your Story

Recently I was conversing with Jesus about the calling of Saul (Paul) of Tarsus. After Saul's dramatic conversion experience on the road to Damascus, Jesus appears in a vision to a disciple named Ananias and tells him to reach out to this notorious persecutor of the church. Ananias is understandably cautious. But Jesus says, "Go! This man is my chosen instrument to proclaim my name to the Gentiles" (Acts 9:15).

I confessed to Jesus that I'd like to be his "chosen instrument" for something. (I said this despite the fact that Jesus's next line about Saul is, "I will show him how much he must suffer for my name"!) I wondered about the nature of a calling. Are we indeed called to something specific? And if so, can we resist or miss our calling? But mostly I just wanted to be Jesus's chosen instrument for some grand mission.

After sitting in silence with Jesus, his response emerged: "You are my chosen instrument to be Robert." I bathed in the affirming love of the moment as I also considered what it really means to "be Robert."

It turns out the answer is yes, we are called to something specific. And yes, we can resist and miss our calling. When we don't become ourselves—through pretending, numbing ourselves, aimlessly wandering, ignoring God's leading, and a number of other avoidance tactics—we are missing our calling, the calling to be ourselves fully alive. You are Jesus's chosen instrument to be you. What does that look like, you fully alive? It's a unique and powerful calling, one that no one else on earth can answer.

Let's do a little experiment with *lectio divina*, the practice of meditative reading in which (in this Ignatian form of the practice) you immerse yourself in a scripture passage or story by engaging your imagination to experience the sights, sounds, smells, and overall reality of the scene.[1] You might be one of the characters in the scene or just yourself as a bystander. There is no right or wrong in this really, just try to make yourself fully present to each scene. Take time with each passage and don't rush on to the next one. They are brief but powerful. They should be short enough for you to read each one and then close your eyes and immerse yourself in it. (Feel free to read the passage in your Bible.) We are going to discuss the scenes, but if you come to understand God communicating something to you, by all means make note of it, prayerfully and meditatively consider it, and act on it.

Scene One (Gen 1:1–3): In the beginning, the earth is something like a watery chaos. The spirit of God moves across the dark, formless abyss, and God says, "Let there be light," and there is light.

Scene Two (Gen 2:7): God makes the human and breathes the breath of life into his nostrils, and "then he became a living being."

Scene Three (Mark 4:35–41): Jesus and some disciples are in a boat. It's evening. The sea gets stormy. The disciples are afraid the boat will go under. Jesus is in the stern, asleep on a cushion. The panicked disciples wake Jesus. He rebukes the wind and says to the sea, "Peace! Be still!" Dead calm. Jesus asks the disciples why they are afraid.

Scene Four (John 20:19–22): It's evening on Easter Sunday. The disciples are huddled together in a house behind locked doors because they're afraid of the authorities. Suddenly, the resurrected Jesus is standing with them. He says to them, "Peace be with you." Then he breathes on them and tells them to "receive the Holy Spirit."

Theses scenes have a number of things in common, but three are particularly important:

1. There is disorder: chaos and darkness, lifelessness, storm, fear.
2. God is intimately present: speaking, breathing, speaking, breathing.
3. God brings order: light and creation, life, calm, peace.

This is the story of the mind.

1. *There is disorder.* You live your story. You have been living it since you were born. (In your family and in the mind and life of God it has been

---

[1]. There are many helpful guides for Ignatian contemplation and *lectio divina*. A good place to start is James Martin's *The Jesuit Guide to (Almost) Everything*, and George Ganss's *The Spiritual Exercises of Ignatius of Loyola*.

going since long before you were born.) But things have happened that have brought disorder to . . .

a. *Your story's setting.* Perhaps there was or is disorder in your home. There is disorder in your community and nation marked by poverty, crime, prejudice, isolation among people, and so on. And there is certainly disorder in the world marked by things like war, ideological clashes, tyranny and oppression, mass poverty, disease, starvation, mass displacement, and alienation.

b. *Your story's lead character.* There is disorder in who you are because of a poorly formed character, because of bad choices, or perhaps because of sin in your life. Maybe you have a deep character flaw that has kept you from making healthy decisions, or that resulted in one particularly bad decision that continues to shape your life. Or perhaps you have a decent character but are drawn to, or even controlled by, something that pulls you away from God and God's best for you and/or your loved ones. Maybe you've just lived like a good-ol'-fashioned sinner: You sometimes do your best, typically follow your appetites, try to be a "good" person, go your own way when it's convenient, and have no real accountability.

c. *Your story's driving force.* The combination of disorder in your setting and in your character contributes to disorder in your driving force. What you are after is misguided or convoluted. It might be outright worldliness and sin—some form of the money, pleasure, and/or power that have taken control of your heart, as we discussed previously. More likely it's seemingly honorable things like a good house, reliable car, money in the bank, good health, and the like. But you can eventually get to the point that, rather than you simply having these things, *they* have *you.* Then, things can easily teeter toward having and being "better," meaning in part, never quite good enough. And also meaning better than others—a better house, better car, more money, better body, more status, better spouse . . . than so-and-so has. All of it is a lifelong exercise in futility if it is what drives us, and even if, like so many, it's our source of security. Any wealth, pleasure, or power—whether grand or modest—will come to an end, and the story and life driven by such pursuits will likewise end.

d. *Your story's genre.* This can be one of the most confusing aspects of living your story. You might be living what the culture considers a love story, but it revolves around feelings of romance and attraction toward others or a specific other. More, it depends on those feelings being returned. Still more, it depends on those feelings being consistently felt and returned basically forever. A love story in which the love doesn't last is not much of a love story. Another complication is the "success story." Someone may heroically go from rags to riches and believe their life to be a success story. But as the big picture is considered or the end draws near, if those riches and worldly successes are all there is, then the story becomes a tragedy. And even the sincere, lifelong love of a significant other comes to an end—it cannot conquer death, despite our romantic notions to the contrary. In this sense, pretty much any story that does not become a *true* love story ends up a chaotic tragedy.

2. *God is intimately present.* In the midst of the chaos around and within you, a still, small voice emerges and asks, "What are you doing here?" (see 1 Kgs 19:12–13). Disorder is not all there is. You are not alone. Like a river that has been running under the ground of your life, God's eternal story begins to spring up. You merge your story with God's story to create a new story. This new story is part of the transformation of your mind as it guides . . .

    a. *Your story's setting.* You identify with Jesus's mission to bring God's kingdom into the world until the earth is "full of the knowledge of the Lord as the waters cover the sea" (Isa 11:9). Your vision is no longer limited to the disorder around you, but instead, you begin to see that this is the landscape for the emergence and presence of God's kingdom. The setting of your story, of your life, becomes God's kingdom coming into your home, your community, your nation, and your world. Or to put it the other way around, your home, your community, your nation, and your world are becoming God's kingdom until "the kingdom of the world has become the kingdom of our Lord and of his Messiah, and he will reign for ever and ever" (Rev 11:15).

    b. *Your story's lead character.* Having recognized the present reality of Jesus's kingdom mission, you begin to intentionally take up your role in fulfilling that mission. You begin to see beyond the material world and recognize the authority of the spiritual reality all around and inside you. This transforms your mind and, thus, your life. Made in God's image, you begin to truly live as a co-creator with God in the world. Your Spirit-empowered apprenticeship to the master, Jesus, begins to grow you, and to grow you up. As an individual and as part of Christ's universal church, you move toward "unity in the faith and in the knowledge of the Son of God and become mature, attaining to the whole measure of the fullness of Christ" (Eph 4:13).

c. *Your story's driving force.* You are now awakening to the mission and likeness of Jesus as they are beginning to be lived in your own being. You see God and God's kingdom within you, as well as all around you, and you realize you are sharing the life of the Trinity. But like a song you are trying to remember, this divine union seems at one moment strong and clear, and the next moment a distant echo. You want to know and sing that song . . . you *have* to know and sing that song. You can't get it out of your head. So you adjust your life to pursue the music, the music of union. It becomes a most satisfying dissatisfaction—simultaneously filled and wanting more.[2] Instead of worldly pursuits (at least for their own sakes), you begin to pursue this union with God, removing whatever doesn't belong. This is eternal life, "the life that is truly life" (1 Tim 6:19).

d. *Your story's genre.* As you come to intimately know this God and merge your story with God's story into a new story, you begin to learn what love truly is. You identify less and less with the tragedies of the world's "love" stories and "success" stories. The paradigm shifts. You begin to live the love story you were made to tell—receiving love, living in love, and sharing love. You are transformed by the reality that, of all the myriad things your

---

2. This is the concept of *epektasis*, described especially in the mystic tradition. God being God and Creator, and humans being creatures, God's capacity for goodness and, well, God-ness is inexhaustible. So the hungry seeker must find satisfaction in dissatisfaction, in tasting God but always wanting more. Gregory of Nyssa wrote, "What Moses yearned for is satisfied by the very things which leave his desire unsatisfied," and Bernard of Clairvaux taught that "even when the soul has found [God] it will not cease to seek him" and "there will be no end to desire, and so no end of seeking." See (respectively) Gregory of Nyssa, *Moses*, number 235, and Bernard of Clairvaux, "Sermon," 84.1, 274.

beautiful life in this wonder-filled world gets to experience and even to live for, "the greatest of these is love" (1 Cor 13:13). That, dear friend, is the making of an epic love story.

3. *God brings order.* This is the nature of God and God's presence. There can be beauty in chaos and disorder, but not in chaos and disorder devoid of hope. In the end it is only God's assuring presence that allows for beauty—for a story—in the midst of chaos. While there may be beauty in the raw stuff of chaos, it is fundamentally the understanding of order that allows for the appreciation of disorder. Picasso and Pollock, Schoenberg and Mingus, Joyce and cummings and Beckett and Cocteau and David Lynch all studied and knew ordered, "proper" art before they began to explore the ordered disorder each became known for. I would go so far as to say it is the hope of order that gives rise to a story in the midst of disorder. The process of turning disorder into order in your story begins in your mind with these three characteristics:

   a. *Peace.* What Jesus says to the stormy sea and to the frightened, hiding disciples, he says to you: "Peace." We've talked about peace as shalom, as well-being and wholeness among God, humanity, self, and creation. This peace is rooted in order. It is ultimately the absence of strife and despair among God and humanity and creation. It does not mean there isn't tension, conflict, even death . . . at least for now. But no matter what is happening in the world around you, you can have an ordered, peaceful mind. Like Jesus in the storm-tossed boat, a mind resting in God is a mind at peace.

   b. *Joy.* The same God who spoke creation into the midst of chaos and who breathed life into the first creation, and after the resurrection breathed life into the new creation, has words and breath for you. We've talked about joy as delight and contentment in the world and in ourselves based on the recognition that God is present in both. This joy is rooted in order. It is the calm assurance that the world, the lives of your loved ones, and your own life are all in God's wise and loving care. No matter what is happening in the world around you, you can have an ordered, joyful mind. Like God bringing light in the darkness, a mind filled with light is a joyful mind.

c. *Love.* The words of disorder (as we are using them here)—chaos, darkness, the unknown, death, fear—describe the story without God. It is when God brings order into the story—creation, light, revelation, life, calm—that there is peace and joy . . . and love. We've talked about love as actively willing and working for the good of others, even at a cost to self. This love is rooted in order. It is the order that comes from life in loving relationship with the Trinity, resting in God's love and joining God in actively loving others.

> This is how we know that we live in him and he in us: He has given us of his Spirit. And we have seen and testify that the Father has sent his Son to be the Savior of the world. If anyone acknowledges that Jesus is the Son of God, God lives in them and they in God. And so we know and rely on the love God has for us. God is love. Whoever lives in love lives in God, and God in them (1 John 4:13-16).

This is your story becoming one with God's story. Herein lies (as it is described by John): God's Spirit given to us; God the Father's generous compassion for his world; God's Son sent as Savior of the world; and us alive in God and God in us, all bound up in love.

And it all comes down to this: "And so we know and rely on the love God has for us." Some translations say, " . . . we have known and believe the love God has for us" (NRSV). But notice how this realization of God's love takes place in the mind—we *know*, we *rely on* or *believe*. This way of thinking transforms our being. Peace, joy, and love come from a mind fully committed to God's love for us. This full knowledge of, reliance on, and belief in God's love is how we come to obey Jesus's command to "love the Lord your God with all your mind." A couple of verses later John writes, "We love because he first loved us" (1 John 4:19). Because we know and believe that God loves us, we can begin to love. The more we love, the more we know of God's love. John Wesley called this verse "the sum of all religion, the genuine model of Christianity."[3] I think he's right. A mind shaped by this perfect love—focused on loving God, resting in God's love, and committed to loving all whom God loves—is flourishing and fruitful. This is what it is to live a story much bigger than anything our minds could ever conceive, because now "we have the mind of Christ" (1 Cor 2:16). Imagine that!

---

3. Wesley, *Notes*, 638.

STEPS ON THE JOURNEY

Learning to Love with Your Whole Mind

1. Prayerfully read and consider Isaiah 55. What does this passage have to do with loving God with your whole mind? What might it mean to have the "mind of Christ"? How do our thoughts and feelings influence who we are and what we do?

2. What part of learning God's story—that God made the world in love, God made all people in love, God loves you, and God wants you to love—do you find most difficult or challenging? Why?

3. What part of living God's story—making yourself at home in the world, making others at home in the world, trusting God's goodness, and sharing God's goodness—do you find most difficult? Why? Where do you see the conflict of nature versus grace in the world? In your life?

4. Name some specific ways in which you have experienced and/or are experiencing the reality that: your own life story is set in God's kingdom; you are made in God's image; you and God are one; you and God are love.

5. What are some of the sources of disorder and chaos—obstacles to receiving and giving love—in your life? Take whatever steps are necessary to remove or overcome these obstacles. This might include seeking counseling, recovery, or therapy, forgiving or making peace with someone, joining a small group in your church, and the like.

6. Plan ways to fill your mind with good, beautiful, noble, and godly thoughts. Some possibilities include:

a. Memorize long passages of scripture, such as Psalms 8 and 23, Isaiah 35 and 55, Matthew 5–7 and John 14–16, Romans 12 and Colossians 3:1–17 and 1 John 4:7–21, or any passages that are meaningful to you. Take whatever time you need, a little bit at a time—you can do it.

b. Employ the method of imaginative reading discussed in chapter 8. Return to one of those passages, or some other, and simply be with it in an unhurried way. Let it saturate your mind.

c. Engage with books, music, films, and art that are of high quality and that help form your mind in positive ways.

d. Spend time with people that inspire, encourage, and intellectually challenge you.

e. Get outside and enjoy the sunlight, fresh air, and beauty of nature.

f. Learn a new subject or skill.

PART III

Strength: Brute Beauty

9

Mirror, Mirror

My family and I were enjoying a rare Sunday morning at home after the busy Advent season and Christmas services. That's when I got the text. It was from my twenty-something choir director, a bright, delightful young lady who, nevertheless, was not one to mince words. "Eunice just went down. I think she's dead." The shock was only slightly curbed by the humor of the text's sudden, frank wording. Also, Eunice was old and had been declining so it wasn't a complete surprise. Still, any such news is troubling, and the fact that it was happening at church—and in my absence—was jarring. And was she, in fact, dead?

We finally got word that Eunice had been taken by ambulance to the hospital. My wife and I headed over. When we arrived we discovered that, yes, Eunice had collapsed on her way out of the sanctuary after worship. And yes, Eunice was dead. One couldn't have scripted a more fitting end for Eunice, a dear soul with a wry sense of humor who was at the church every time the doors were open. Now, here she lay in a cold hospital holding-room in December, having been singing hymns and listening to a sermon only an hour before. Church members began to peel away to get some lunch and continue with their Sunday naps and football viewing. The remaining member told us that Eunice's kids were coming from a town a few hours away. We insisted this lady go on home and we would wait for the family.

So there Jamie and I sat, with Eunice's lifeless body between us, for several hours. As a pastor I was somewhat used to being around the departing and very-recently-departed. Within my first few months as a pastor a family called me to pray with them in the hospital room of their dead mother. They asked if we could all hold hands, including my holding the dead mother's hand, which was still slightly warm yet was also cooling and stiffening and very clearly devoid of life. It's an indescribable and unforgettable feeling. But a number of similar incidents followed over the years and, while I'm always sensitive to and mystified by the dying and dead, it was no longer a novelty. But Jamie was fascinated. She has always had a childlike curiosity and enthusiasm. And she loved Eunice. So she held Eunice's hand, looked closely at her face, and wondered aloud to me about Eunice's present state of being, as she was clearly no longer living in the earthly tent that had housed her for eighty-odd years.

Our culture used to be much more familiar with death. Parents, grandparents, and all too often even children, died at home. We didn't have today's medical and end-of-life care, of course, which are a great blessing to many. But we also didn't go to such extensive and expensive lengths to keep death out of our lives. By the time most people reached adulthood they likely had seen up-close-and-personal at least one person die. My point is this: Death gives us perspective. Not the bloodlust kind of death that characterizes the worst aspects of our culture, but watching someone we know as alive suddenly no longer be. They still look the same but they're no longer here. It teaches us something about the fragility of life and opens us to the mysteries of death. But it also invites us to a balanced understanding of life in these mortal bodies. What are we to make of these fleshly, often troublesome miracles that house us for a time . . . and then don't (and then one day are resurrected to house us forever—whatever *that* might mean)?

Many people begin a new year with resolutions. By the end of January some are just taking off, some are flying high, and some have crashed and burned. Whatever your experience has been with resolutions, any survey would reveal that the vast majority of New Year's resolutions would come under the heading of "Body." There are certainly strong psychological and spiritual connections, but the body is the battleground. Lose weight, eat healthier, exercise, stop smoking, and even things like manage stress and travel more are typically part of getting some kind of control over our bodily experience of life. So why are our bodies always causing us so much trouble?

First, the good news: Our bodies are the source of an immeasurable amount of pleasure. Everything from food, sex, work, and vacations, to hearing great music, smelling springtime, tasting chocolate, playing games with our children, and looking at a sunset or the stars or a painting or the mountains or a loved one, all these and so much more are experienced through our bodies.

Then, there's the bad news: Our bodies are the source of an immeasurable amount of pain. Everything from injury, disability, abuse, and disease, to adultery, starvation, homelessness, imprisonment, addiction, war, slavery, and so much more bad and even evil are all experienced through our bodies. So, is the body good or bad . . . or downright evil?

One of the deepest and most consistent misunderstandings in the history of the Christian faith is the nature of the body. Even in Christianity's first years, the heresy of early forms of Gnosticism threatened and deceived many Christians. It taught that the physical world is evil, that Jesus was either purely a spirit being or only a human who had secret knowledge that made him divine, and that the goal of spirituality and faith is to escape physical existence. Parts of this seem absurd, but parts seem very much in keeping with what we think of as Christian belief, even possibly taught in the Bible. Doesn't the Bible, and Paul especially, say all kinds of things about how we need to take control of our bodies because the flesh is evil, about how we need to overcome the body and live a mostly spiritual existence until we transcend it all and move on to a purely spiritual plane . . . or something like that? The answer is yes and no. We do need to exercise control over our bodies and to nurture the spiritual aspects of life. But it's not because our flesh is evil, and the goal is certainly not to escape the flesh. On the contrary.

Two of the most important concepts in all of scripture are given to us by John the Evangelist right at the outset of his Gospel. The first is this: All creation, including the material world and our bodies, came into being through Jesus Christ, the Word of God (see John 1:3). From the creation story in Genesis right through to the story of new creation inaugurated with Jesus's resurrection, we see God creating the world and humanity on purpose, as the result of God's good and perfect will. This physical and fleshly creation is light, not darkness, and it is life, not death. God is not surprised, confused, or disappointed that there is a physical world or that we have flesh. God willed and spoke it all into being.

And the second vital scriptural concept that John gives us is this: This Word of God who created the world of matter and flesh, actually became matter and flesh (1:14). The incarnation of the Son of God is the single most important statement about the nature of the physical world. The fact that God, the essence of holiness and purity, became a fully flesh-and-blood human—exactly like us in every way, including temptation, yet without sin (Heb 4:15)—perfectly illustrates that our bodies are not evil. You might say,

"Well, God took on a body so he could save us from the evil of our flesh. Because our flesh is evil, God had to take on flesh so he could sacrifice himself and deliver us from the evils of the material world." There are parts of that somewhat common belief that are loosely connected to the history of Christian theology and have a hint of truth to them. But there's a big problem here: the resurrection. Jesus, the Son of God, was a fully flesh-and-blood human who lived a real flesh life and died a real flesh death. But then he was resurrected as real flesh . . . still. He wasn't resurrected as a ghost in heaven, but as his real flesh self on earth. Was there something different about the nature of his resurrected body? That seems to be the mysterious case. But the difference was not that he was no longer flesh. In fact, as far as we know, he is *still* flesh. Let that sink in for a moment.

So, our bodies are not bad—or evil—despite how things might often seem. Do our bodies fail us? Yes. Will our bodies ultimately fail us? Yes, at least in this life as we know it. Does this mean we should pay no attention to our bodies? Or does this mean we should pay ultimate attention to our bodies? Or, rather than our bodies failing us, might it be more accurate to say that we fail our bodies? More on these matters to come.

But for now, a helpful thing would be to acknowledge our bodies. They often don't give us much choice, with their appetites and pains. But there are healthy ways to intentionally acknowledge your body. First, be aware of God's goodness that you experience through your body: good food, good sex, good music, work and play and exercise, movement from place to place, interaction with other people, and on and on. Second, try thanking God every day for some part of your body, including something you've experienced as a result of it. It might be a fond memory of an experience from long ago. Or it might just be your everyday life: a mouth for speaking or kissing, hands for work or a hobby, ears for hearing your children laughing, rest after a day of working. And finally, not for the faint of heart, look at your body—in the mirror or in person, clothed or unclothed, whatever you can handle. Begin to accept your body. Marvel at it, laugh at it, or simply be aware of it. You might be working to improve it, and that's fine and good. But thank God that he became flesh like you. And thank God that he made you who you are and loves you as you are.

God's love for our bodies is an example of his grace and mercy. God doesn't need you to look a certain way before he gives you his attention. God doesn't turn his attention to someone else once you stop looking or functioning a certain way. God doesn't turn away because of your bodily sins of the past . . . or the present. Like a parent doting on their child's beauty, God thinks your body is beautiful. And God has loving, beautiful plans for your body. The trick is to not let a misguided heart and mind get in the way. Accepting your body, and accepting that God accepts your body, is a strong beginning. But it's only the beginning.

10

The King is Dead

I was a king. I had a kingdom. I inherited my kingdom when I was just a child. I wasn't crowned king of my kingdom in some grand ceremony. It was a gradual coronation. My kingdom grew as I learned that my kingdom could get me things—food, fun, affection—and that my kingdom could control other people—mostly my family, then a few friends. Sometimes, though, my kingdom failed to obtain for me the things I wanted or to enable me to control others the way I, the king, saw fit. This weakness in my kingdom resulted in two primary things: first, it made me want the pleasures and control even more. And second, I began to devise alternate ways of getting that pleasure and control. As I became a teenager and then an adult my reign only grew mightier. Like any thriving kingdom throughout history, my kingdom's demand for pleasure and need for control grew stronger. And, like any thriving kingdom, my kingdom's influence and ability to obtain pleasure and control also grew stronger. In fact, today my kingdom's capacity for pleasure and control is probably the strongest it's ever been.

But, as I mentioned, I *was* a king. On the road to today two things happened that ended up toppling my kingdom. First, I realized that my kingdom—all six feet seven inches, 210 pounds of it—is going to die after only a few decades (maybe sooner), and there's absolutely nothing I can do about that. And second, I met a king who is far more powerful than I, and whose kingdom will never die. So I surrendered. Well, I mostly surrendered. That's my problem. In some ways, the reality that my kingdom is going to die drives me to cling even more tightly to it. But the more preoccupied I am with my six-feet-seven-inch kingdom, which is really already as good as dead, the more I cut myself off from the king and kingdom that will never die. And the most beautiful and tragic part of the whole story is, this king offers me *his* kingdom. I just need to give up my own.

This is how the apostle Paul tells that same story:

> Those who live according to the flesh have their minds set on what the flesh desires; but those who live in accordance with the Spirit have their minds set on what the Spirit desires. The mind governed by the flesh is death, but the mind governed by the Spirit is life and peace. The mind governed by the flesh is hostile to God; it does not submit to God's law, nor can it do so. Those who are in the realm of the flesh cannot please God (Rom 8:5–8).

It is not the body that keeps us from God or even generates sin in our lives. It is when we choose (via a misguided heart and mind) to cling to our bodies as our kingdom that we cut ourselves off from the life and peace of God and God's kingdom.

The trouble we experience from our bodies is the result of a clash of kingdoms. I like the way Paul words it: "Those who are in the realm of the flesh cannot please God." It isn't just our bodies that are the problem—it's *the realm of the flesh*, the kingdom ruled (in large part) by the body.[1] It is possible to live fully in the body, to experience all its pains and temptations, and yet fully please God and experience God's life and peace. Not only is this possible, this is God's plan. But when we are consumed with our body—whether through pain or pleasure—especially as those without hope, we are left with nothing but the death of our body that is ultimately coming our way. When we continue to focus our lives on those early childhood experiences of pleasure and control exercised through our bodies, we never let go of our kingdom. It just grows and grows, its needs more complicated and its reach more widespread and profound and potentially devastating.

---

1. Paul's use of flesh (*sarx*) here is part of his larger argument distinguishing, essentially, between two kingdoms, the realm of the flesh and the realm of the Spirit. Moo explains that "flesh," in this sense, "is not part of the person, nor even exactly an impulse or 'nature' within the person . . . but a 'power-sphere' in which a person lives." Moo, *Romans*, 418 n. 51. He goes on to equate being "in the flesh" with the non-Christian state, and being "in the Spirit" with the Christian. Ibid., 486. Further, it is important to note that all of this is distinguished from "body" (*sōma*), which "may be the physical body; but it is probably . . . the whole person, viewed in terms of the person's interaction with the world." Ibid., 383. I am more focused here on the Christian's behavior in and orientation toward the body, rather than the overall presence or absence of saving faith. Nevertheless, Moo's descriptions of the flesh as "power sphere" and the body as "interaction with the world" are informative.

We continue throughout our lives—and this, I believe, is the case for the vast majority of people—exalting the kingdom of the body over the kingdom of God. And of course, this is not lived out only in illicit sins of the flesh. The kingdom of the body includes good things like work and health and even family. These are holy things and worthy of our attention and investment. But they are not building blocks for our own kingdom, more and more ways for us to exercise our reign. When this bodily life that we build for ourselves apart from God comes to its end, what then? We find that we really died a long time ago.

This, of course, is not only my story. Your kingdom might not be six feet seven and 210 pounds, but you have a kingdom. You know your kingdom's appetites for pleasure and control, even as they are manifested in good forms like work, health, and relationships. You've likely encountered the same threats to your kingdom: death and the kingdom of God. Perhaps you've fully surrendered. Perhaps you struggle, sometimes letting go and experiencing the life and peace of God's Spirit and God's kingdom, and sometimes fighting for control and for the kingdom of your body. And perhaps you never knew. You're just building life in the body the way the world tells you to, helpless and hopeless in the face of temptation, pain, and death.

But just as you and I have in common the tragic story of our doomed kingdoms, we also potentially share the happy ending. The king offers *you* his kingdom. And the amazing thing is, you don't have to die to get it. This is the sad misunderstanding of many people of faith, thinking that we are imprisoned in our bodies until we finally die and go to God's kingdom. But listen to how Paul continues:

> You, however, are not in the realm of the flesh but are in the realm of the Spirit, if indeed the Spirit of God lives in you . . . [I]f Christ is in you, then even though your body is subject to death because of sin, the Spirit gives life because of righteousness. And if the Spirit of him who raised Jesus from the dead is living in you, he who raised Christ from the dead will also give life to your mortal bodies because of his Spirit who lives in you (Rom 8:9-11).

This is not only payable on death—this is now. The same way living for the doomed kingdom of the body makes us as good as dead already, so living for the eternal kingdom of God gives us life already. As we learn to look at and acknowledge and accept our bodies, including the fleshly temptations and physical pain and bodily death that are all too real, we can take comfort in knowing that we are more than what we see. We *were* kings and queens, yes, but of doomed kingdoms. Now we are children of God, the king who will never die, and whose kingdom will never end and has come into our very bodies. Our bodies, his kingdom. That's amazing news to be celebrated, and celebrated by living an abundant bodily life. Long live the king!

11

The Power of the Temple, or How to Get Punched Out

I've been punched a number of times in my life. But I've been punched out only once. I was twenty-two. There were a couple of skater punks who had begun attending the youth group I was working with. By their own testimony, they originally came for the girls but ended up staying for Jesus. One summer night my friend Kiley and I were hanging out in a bowling alley parking lot with these kids and another skater friend they'd begun bringing to church. We were debating whether or not to go in and bowl as we stood around Kiley's pickup listening to music and talking and laughing together.

Suddenly a jeep full of teenagers sped through the parking lot, followed closely by another couple of cars. The boys were visibly shaken and said we should all get out of there. I asked why and they said the guys in those cars were always picking fights with them. In a flash of courage, pride, ego, and stupidity, I insisted we weren't going anywhere. We were there first and had the right to be in that lovely bowling alley parking lot if we wanted. Besides, they hadn't even stopped . . . yet.

They drove on through and pulled into the parking lot of the K-Mart across the street. The three cars' headlights flashed on us, and now they were joined by another couple of cars. The boys kept urging us all to leave. But I was determined to teach them that they didn't have to be afraid and they didn't have to fight—"Blessed are the peacemakers" and all that. And maybe those guys were just going to hang out in the K-Mart parking lot, right? Wrong. A couple dozen teenagers poured out of the cars and started across the street toward us. A lot of them looked my age. There were a few girls but most of them were guys, many in tank tops that showed off their huge arms and necks. Now, I'm a big dude, but I'm not twenty big dudes. My heart raced. *Here we go*, I thought. *It's on.* But I only muttered through clenched teeth for everyone to stay calm.

The crowd assembled around the five of us. There was a feigned casualness as everyone pretended nothing was about to happen. I made a joke to my group and we laughed. A fidgety, twitchy muscle-head stepped forward and asked me what I was laughing at. I'd been around enough picked fights growing up to know that that's what was now happening. So I rolled my eyes and got on with it.

"I was just joking with my friends here," I said.

Twitchy was several inches shorter than me but was all muscles and veins. He had crazy eyes and was obviously on something. "I don't think it's funny," he said.

"So?" I said, still laughing. I was determined not to stop laughing, trying to convey the absurdity of it all.

"So you wanna go?" he said. At this point a bulldog-shaped guy stepped up next to him.

"Why?" I asked.

"Cuz you're bigger 'n me," he replied, flexing his neck.

"So?" I said again, still laughing and straining to find the logic.

"So you wanna go?" he insisted.

"Why?" I asked again, probing for a better answer. To no avail.

"Cuz you're bigger 'n me!"

I laughed and said, "I think we've established that." My group laughed. I looked over at them and shrugged. Bad idea. Never look away from someone who is picking a fight with you. Maybe you knew that. I did not.

Twitchy's fist felt like a baseball bat against my temple. Everything went black. Then what felt like a brick slammed against my mouth. I could feel myself rocking back and forth. In a split second I debated whether or not to try and stabilize myself. But I knew if I stayed up this was going to get out of hand. I could take a punch or two, by God's grace. But any more and I would probably lose it. So I took a dive. In the name of Jesus, Gandhi, Martin Luther King, and my mother, I went down like a big sack of potatoes. Twitchy and Bulldog (who I later found out had thrown the second punch) taunted me to get up. Kiley kept offering me his hand to help me up, but I waved it off. I just sat there laughing. (I hadn't yet realized I had blood covering my teeth and face and all down the front of my shirt.)

PART III—STRENGTH: BRUTE BEAUTY

The owner of the bowling alley came out and yelled that he had called the police. Everybody ran across the street and sped off. A couple of girls remained and kept apologizing and asking if I wanted them to take me to the hospital. I thanked them and declined, wondering why they thought I needed to go to the hospital. The boys left and Kiley and I went to his house. That's when I saw my gruesome, blood-soaked self in the mirror. That's also when I put some ice chips inside my lower lip only to discover water dripping *through* my lip and out the other side. Thanks to Bulldog's class ring and my own teeth, I now had a hole through my lower lip. So Kiley and I ended up at the emergency room. Another fun night of youth ministry.

I've carried this memory (and a few painful others) over the years as a reminder of the conflict of kingdoms and how the body is often the battleground. The fight is also waged in our hearts and minds, of course. But the body is typically where it is lived out. My heart wanted to make peace. My mind debated the "fight or flight" instinct and decided on neither, or maybe on a different kind of fight. But it was my body that had to serve as the example to these young Christians of what it actually looks like to will peace and choose love. Whether or not there is a time for Christians to hit back can be debated. But in this case there needed to be an example of a break with the former, pre-Christian way of living. It wasn't a perfect example. But the lesson was conveyed. The boys consistently chose non-violence in subsequent confrontations, and the bullies—who, it turns out, were raging nineteen-year-old steroid users and dealers—eventually left them alone. The skaters who had come for the girls but found Jesus were now becoming disciples. And the scar I still have on my lip was totally worth it.

The body can rightly be described as a battleground. Countless others have fought much more important and impactful fights than mine, and at much greater cost. But this battleground view of the body shouldn't be the end and isn't God's ultimate intention for it. Or another way of considering it is that the body is a battleground for a reason: it possesses an extraordinary treasure. Our bodies are made to be profoundly powerful, complex, and sacred houses. And what they house is far more powerful, complex, and sacred. And that's what we fight for. Our bodies are the spatiotemporal geography of our present experience of life. But they are not the sum total of our life. Temptations and conflicts will come and go as part of bodily life as we now know it. But there is more to bodily life than fending off—and occasionally surrendering to—sin. Much more.

THE POWER OF THE TEMPLE, OR HOW TO GET PUNCHED OUT

What are some of your favorite foods? Imagine you can no longer eat those foods but have to eat just to stay alive, only consuming the same very basic meal every day. What are your favorite clothes? How much did you think about your outfit today? Imagine you have to wear the same very simple clothes every day. While there are many people in the world who have no choice about such matters, many others who do have a choice still choose simple meals and simple clothing. It can be easier to make healthy eating choices by sticking to a consistent, basic diet and only occasionally splurging. And many people, from artists and musicians to CEOs and scientists and even world-famous fashion designers choose a simple daily uniform, claiming it frees them to focus their thinking on other matters. And both simple eating and simple dressing can make it easier to be sure we are buying only from those who are committed to fair and just farming and manufacturing practices. Of course, simplicity is not necessarily required for such commitments; it just makes things . . . simpler.

These seem like trivial things to many. Hopefully you aren't in a situation where you really *have* to worry about these things, whether or not you'll have clothes to put on or enough food to eat today. We must be mindful of and compassionate toward those who face such hardships. It's a luxury to get to choose between simplicity and complexity, a choice the majority of the world doesn't have. And we must do all we can to ensure everyone at least has simple, regular nourishment and clothing. But Jesus is talking about so much more when he talks about how God takes care of the "birds of the air" and the "flowers of the field" (Matt 6:25–34). Jesus is talking about the clash of kingdoms: the kingdom of the body versus the kingdom of God. Not surprisingly, Jesus comes down firmly on the side of the kingdom of God. Curiously, though, he uses the material world and the body as examples of the compassionate care of God's kingdom. Does Jesus's choice of God's kingdom over our bodily kingdom mean God views our bodies as something only to be fought and transcended? Or could it be that the two kingdoms not only are *not* mutually exclusive but can actually support one another?

Jesus teaches us not to worry about what we'll eat or what we'll wear, but to seek first God's kingdom (verses 31–33). But does that mean he thinks the body is unimportant? No. He is saying the body is not all-important, but he is not saying the body is unimportant. In fact, the body is our vehicle or vessel for experiencing and serving and glorifying God, and for helping others to experience and serve and glorify God. While we certainly come to know and love God with the unseen parts of our lives like our hearts, our minds, and our souls, we also come to know and love God in very significant ways with the visible part of our lives, including our bodies.

The body is so important in our relationship with God that the apostle Paul says our bodies are God's temple. He says this a couple of different times. Once, he uses the second-person plural, speaking about the church: "Do y'all not know that y'all are God's temple and the Holy Spirit dwells in y'all?" (1 Cor 3:17; if Bible translators would get on board with us southerners, things would be a lot clearer). But the other time, speaking clearly about avoiding sins of the flesh, Paul says to individuals, "Do you not know that your bodies are temples of the Holy Spirit, who is in you, whom you have received from God? You are not your own; you were bought at a price. Therefore honor God with your bodies" (1 Cor 6:19–20). It doesn't get much clearer than that.

So, we've come to understand that our bodies are not bad or evil. We've also come to understand that our bodies are not our kingdoms to be obsessed over for our selfish purposes, but that we should seek God's kingdom in our bodies. In fact, Paul's instruction that we are not our own but have been bought at a price sounds like a battle over our bodies has already been fought and won. But what does this mean? What does it mean to be a temple of the Holy Spirit and to "honor God with your bodies"?

Consider the temple of your body in light of the actual Jewish temple, the building that was the center of worship for God's people for many generations. First, the temple was where God was encountered in power. Paul says your body is a temple of the Holy Spirit. We take that for granted, so take a moment and let that sink in: Your body houses God the Holy Spirit, who is just as divine as God the Father and God the Son. Jesus promised, "You will receive power when the Holy Spirit comes on you" (Acts 1:8). So Jesus is essentially saying the result of being a temple of the Holy Spirit is power.

But power for what? Power to obtain material wealth or influence or whatever our hearts might desire? No, Jesus is specific about the Holy Spirit giving us power with a purpose. And the purpose of this power is to bear witness to God's presence. The Holy Spirit continues Jesus's ministry. Jesus says the result of our being joined to the Holy Spirit—which presently happens in our bodies—is that we will be his witnesses. A witness, of course, is someone who has encountered something firsthand. So, to be a temple of the Holy Spirit is to have the power both to encounter Jesus firsthand

and to share this encounter and its ramifications with others. This includes the power of forgiveness—living a life not bearing the weight of guilt, and helping others to lay down that weight. And it includes the power of wholeness—becoming the fully-alive person God intends you to be, and helping others to become their God-intended selves. This and so much more is what happens when God is encountered in power.

Second, the temple was where God was sacrificially worshiped. Paul wrote that we should "offer your bodies as a living sacrifice, holy and pleasing to God—this is true worship" (Rom 12:1). This is the giving of yourself fully, including your body, to God and God's will. Such a worshipful lifestyle is called holiness. God's holiness is God's mysterious and matchless glory and worth, deserving of our worship. Our holiness, then, is living a life that faithfully expresses God's glory and worth. Holy living is letting go of false gods (including yourself and your body) and yielding to the true God alone. In the arts it takes a lot of effort for things to seem effortless. Years of disciplined practice precede what appear to be off-the-cuff performances and the seemingly natural mastery of a craft. And so it is in the life of faith. It takes a lot of disciplined practice for us to yield to and show forth God's glory in the midst of each day's busy energy and competing agendas.

Using Jesus's example of food and clothes—that life is more than what we wear and eat—such discipline might include modesty in dress and moderation in consuming. It might include things like regular fasting, or regular times in silence and solitude, or simplicity in what we consume and faithfulness in where we obtain it, or other ways of bringing aspects of bodily life into worshipful submission to God. Such disciplines are not to prove something to God or others. And they are not merely to strengthen our will power. We can't become fully surrendered, powerful temples of the Holy Spirit simply by our own will power, any more than a gardener can make things grow simply by willing it. But that gardener can do a number of things to cultivate and facilitate the garden's growth. Likewise, there are many things we can do to become a more faithful dwelling place for God and vessel for God's purposes. A life of such sacrificial worship will yield growth in holiness—a life more clearly experiencing and expressing God's mysterious, fiery beauty.

Finally, the temple was where heaven and earth intersected. Jesus taught his followers to pray for God's kingdom to come on earth as it is in heaven. When we see Jesus bringing God's kingdom rule into the world, we see him doing this in his body and by impacting bodily lives (which, of course, ends up impacting all of life). Sometimes Jesus is doing more obvious things like healing the sick and raising the dead. But when, for example, Jesus encounters the rich man who wants to know what good thing he must do to inherit eternal life, Jesus eventually tells him to sell his possessions, give the money to the poor, and then to come and follow him (see Mark 10:17–22). The reason this proposition ultimately proves unacceptable to this man is that he is focused fully on the kingdom of the body—in his case, material wealth.

And that leads us to a vital understanding I must make mention of, though I've decided not to make it an entire chapter (and it could fill volumes). When Jesus tells us to love God with our whole strength, his meaning includes our material wealth and our power in the world. Strength is not merely the body itself, but includes all aspects of bodily life. We are to love God with our work, our property, and our money. And we are to love God with our leadership roles and the social influence we have, with our voice and vote and efforts in building communities of shalom. All of this and more constitutes our strength. And all of it is to be held loosely and humbly before the Lord. It is all to be available for God's good. And it is all the result of God's goodness and is a tool for God's goodness to be worked into the lives of others.

So Jesus says don't get hung up on the ordinary things of the body—feeding it, clothing it, housing it, driving it around, satisfying its various appetites. God will see that these things are sufficiently taken care of. Focus instead on the *extra*ordinary things of the body—using it to bring God's kingdom into the world and all that consists of: loving, serving, healing, participating in beauty, joy, justice, and peace. In short, the body is a means to the end of glorifying and enjoying God by exercising his will in and for the world. God's plan for you is not just to get you into heaven when you die. God's plan is to get heaven into you (and, through you, into the world) now. This is what it is to be a temple of the Holy Spirit: that you become a place where heaven and earth intersect.

In the end, some might glorify God in the body by fasting, some by feasting. Some might glorify God in the body with humble coverings, some with *haute couture*. The point is that the body is more than such things. The body fulfills its true purpose when it becomes a temple of "brute beauty,"[1] the fragile, humble place where God is encountered in power, where God is sacrificially worshiped, where heaven comes to earth.

---

1. See Gerard Manley Hopkins, "The Windhover."

THE POWER OF THE TEMPLE, OR HOW TO GET PUNCHED OUT

Imagine living such a life! Seriously. Begin to imagine what your bodily life would be like, not merely as a battleground but as holy ground, as God's temple. And now, in the power of the indwelling Holy Spirit, live abundantly with God in that temple.

12

Armchair Quarterbacks

If you're like me, one thing you experience when watching football on TV is the frustration of knowing how to play better than the guys on the field. Almost every time a pass or tackle are missed or the quarterback gets sacked, I get so frustrated because I could see clearly what needed to happen, while these so-called "professionals" blow it. Of course I have the benefit of dozens of cameras giving me the perspective of the entire field from every conceivable angle. But still, surely I could do better.

The truth is it's hard. Whatever the sport, it's easy to sit at home or in the stands and think we could do better, because the athletes make it look easy. It's the same with music. Every other yahoo in school or at work thinks he or she should be a music superstar because professional musicians make it seem so easy, and they seem like they're having so much fun. It can't be that hard. Or acting. They're just standing there saying words. I do that all the time. And this could be the case for most disciplines. People doing things they love and have diligently practiced make it look so easy and even fun. The next time you're having surgery, maybe I'll sneak in and take over. All I need is a scalpel, right?

It takes a lot more than just the tools. It even takes more than talent. It takes things like a big-picture perspective, disciplined practice, and a deep sense of purpose to lift someone with a decent amount of talent and set them on the road to excellence, to making it look easy. This also happens to be the case with life in the body. We've come to understand that our bodies are not bad or evil, but are good creations of our good God. They are not kingdoms for us to build a life apart from God. Our bodily life is rightly aligned when we open our bodies to become temples of the Holy Spirit, each body a place where God and God's kingdom are coming into the world. But, like a barrage of 300-pound linemen blitzing a quarterback, there seem to be fleshly temptations and physical infirmities and even death constantly closing in on our bodies. And while those may be part of the reality in which we presently live, there are these three things that can help us live in the flesh without being dominated by the flesh—that can help us be, as we might say, comfortable in our own skin.

The first is *perspective*. At the beginning of a season, you don't typically hear an athlete say they want a better endorsement deal (though their agent might hear them say that). You don't hear them say they want to be the best player at their position. You don't even hear them say they want to win games or win their division. What you hear athletes say at the beginning of a season is they want to win the championship. Of course this happens one game at a time, one play at a time, but the goal is to win it all. For a violinist it might be Tchaikovsky's *Violin Concerto in D*; for an actor, *Hamlet*. Whatever the case, the best keep their eyes on the prize.

Regarding the life of the body, Paul wrote, "Don't you realize that in a race everyone runs, but only one person gets the prize? So run to win!" (1 Cor 9:24, NLT). Run to win! Keep your eyes on the prize! Paul goes on to say athletes compete for a prize that fades away, but we are running after an eternal prize. What we are after is life with God. This is the prize that never fades. No temptation, no infirmity, not even death can take away that prize. And no worldly success can compete with that. Our life with God is all that lasts. And while it is not dependent on our bodies, it is currently experienced in our bodies. So that's our championship perspective: Everything we do in, with, and through our bodies must be striving toward the goal of life with God.

The second key to a balanced bodily life is *practice*. It probably goes without saying that those athletes or musicians or surgeons that make what they do look so easy got to that point through years of practice. Malcolm Gladwell wrote in his book *Outliers* about a study that concluded that it takes, on average, ten thousand hours of doing something to attain mastery. There are different views regarding to what degree innate talent is needed to begin with. But whatever the case, excellence takes years of focused work. Yet we think our spiritual lives are different. We think that the moment we decide to follow Christ, God comes in and zaps us holy. Or we think we'd better just hide in a corner of religious do's and don'ts until we die, and then we'll get a heavenly zapping. But in Jesus's life and teaching, and throughout the history of the faith, we see those who are constantly confronted with temptation, pain, and death, yet they seem to move through it with ease.

But it wasn't easy. It took practice. Paul continues with his athletic analogy: "I discipline my body like an athlete, training it to do what it should. Otherwise, I fear that after preaching to others I myself might be disqualified" (verse 27). We train our bodies for godliness when we choose modesty in things like our clothes or car or house, and when we choose moderation in our eating and drinking. We train our bodies when we regularly abstain from food and/or other bodily pleasures for a period, and when we spend regular time in silence and solitude. And there are many such things like exercising, serving, playing, resting, and even simply being present to others that are ways of training our bodies so they'll be and do what God requires of us. This is our championship practice: Everything we do in, with, and through our bodies must be training for our life with God.

And the third key to living *in* the flesh but not *of* the flesh is *purpose*. Professional athletes, musicians, or masters of almost any discipline did not get where they are without knowing their purpose. Athletes push through pain, fatigue, and defeat after defeat because of one thing: they get to play the game. Musicians spend hour after hour alone with their instrument, year after year and maybe a lifetime playing low-paying gigs for unappreciative audiences for one reason: they get to make music. And across disciplines the drive is to excel and to achieve mastery.

Again, Paul writes, "So I run with purpose in every step. I am not just shadowboxing" (verse 26). This is perhaps the place where our bodily life gets most out of balance. We don't know our purpose, so we accept the purpose given to us by the world: the desires of the flesh, the desires of the eyes, and the pride of life (see 1 John 2:15–17). Whether living for obvious sins of the flesh or less obvious worldly successes, in the end it's all the same: shadowboxing, punching at the air. It's confusing because worldly life and the realm of the flesh can seem so much more purposeful than spiritual life and the realm of the Spirit. It's why you must be clear about your purpose to become your fully alive, God-glorifying true self. And you live out that purpose in and through your body as you love the Lord your God with all your strength. You will and work for God's good, God's kingdom, God's shalom, in and through your body. This is our championship purpose: Everything we do in, with, and through our bodies is living out our life with God.

So here we are, in the flesh. Are you comfortable in your own skin? When you look at your perspective—how you see your life's focus or goal—what prize are you reaching for? When you consider your daily practices, what are you training for? When you look at the life you're living and the world around you, what is your purpose? If you are unclear or misguided about any of these, your bodily life is missing passes and getting sacked. You are ruling a doomed kingdom. You are a temple whose god is your belly (see Phil 3:19).

Ours is a culture that worships the body and bodily life. Our religion is materialism, so we shop for and consume whatever props up the bodily being we're so inextricably attached to. Ironically, many of the ways we worship our bodies—such as casual sex, overindulgence in food or drink, obsessive dieting and exercise and cosmetic procedures and preening—can often be harmful to our bodies, especially in light of God's glorious intentions for them. Then we sanitize bodily death and shove it into sterile buildings to get it out of our living rooms and bedrooms, where it was only a century ago, so we can perpetuate the self-delusion that the body will go on forever.

But these bodies as we know them will end. So what if all we know of life is this body? There must be more. And of course there is . . . much more. But for now we experience this "much more" in our bodies—sometimes through our bodies, sometimes in spite of our bodies, but always in our bodies. We do well to find peace in this tension of being *in* the flesh but not *of* the flesh, to experience the fullness of bodily life and then to courageously let it go and move on to other things, with our real life fully in tact.

STEPS ON THE JOURNEY

Learning to Love with Your Whole Strength

1. Prayerfully read and consider Romans 8. What does this passage have to do with loving God with all your strength, with life in and through your body? Why do people often consider the body evil, opposed to God, and something to be escaped?

2. Name three things you like about your body. Write a list of the top ten things you experience or have experienced through your body. Then, keep adding to that list. Take a week and find one thing each day to do in your body that you will thoroughly enjoy. Then thank God for that experience before going to bed.

3. Begin to be more conscientious about your bodily life. Get informed about where things like your food and clothing come from. Consider simplifying—at least for designated periods like Lent or certain days—what you wear and what you eat.

4. Develop healthy perspectives, practices, and purposes for your bodily life. Find the right balance for your body of practices like consuming, fasting, exercising, resting, working, playing, and so on. Begin listening and attending to your body, especially its needs for things like sleep, water, sunlight, fresh air, and touch.

5. Consider Jesus's teaching in Matthew 6:24–34. In what specific ways do you worry about your life and your body? Take advantage of (or create) opportunities to invest things like your wealth, your influence, your possessions, and your body in God's kingdom work.

6. If your eternal destiny is physical—living in a resurrected body and a redeemed creation—how should that affect your life and world now? What specific steps can you take to live that sort of life now?

PART IV

Soul: Deep Like Rivers

13

Take Me to the River

The title of this section, "Deep Like Rivers," comes from the 1920 Langston Hughes poem "The Negro Speaks of Rivers." In this poem, the narrator speaks of the African-American experience as marked by rivers—from the birth of humanity beside the Euphrates and ruling civilizations along the Congo and Nile in Africa, to being enslaved along the Mississippi in the American south. These rivers serve as geographical markers mapping the journey of the narrator's people. But the rivers also serve as a metaphor for the journey of the people's soul. The journey through miles and centuries and profound struggles has caused the soul of the people to grow deep like the rivers that have defined it.

The image of a river is a common metaphor for the soul in poems, stories, songs, and scriptures. The way rivers help nourish and sustain life, define borders, and yet remain somewhat mysterious and independent of us, makes them apt pictures of the soul. The soul, too, nourishes and sustains life, defines borders, and yet remains mysterious and seemingly independent of us. The psalmist, for example, addresses his own soul as if it's another person: "Bless the Lord, O my soul . . . " (Ps 103:1 NRSV). The soul seems so independent of us that it is often neglected, and so it begins to dry up. When rivers dry up, borders begin to erode and life begins to die. And so it is with the soul. A dried-up soul leads to a fragmented self and, ultimately, to death. What can be done about this? One must begin to dig deeper and reconnect to the source.

It seems shockingly appropriate that the first place we meet Jesus in Mark's fast-paced gospel is (where else?) a river. "At that time Jesus came from Nazareth in Galilee and was baptized by John in the Jordan" (Mark 1:9). This, of course, is not just any river. The Jordan is the river that marked the border into the Promised Land. So John the Baptizer, in his ministry of repentance and renewal, is calling Israel back to the beginning, to remember who they are as God's people. And then Jesus comes on the scene and takes that call to a new level, a soul level, a deep-like-rivers level.

God had identified Israel as God's firstborn and beloved son (Exod 4:22; Hos 11:1). This was an identity with which God's set-apart people had struggled throughout their history. Now, instead of the river symbolizing God's life-giving mercy and faithful deliverance, it had come to be a symbol of political identity and threatened national boundaries. This is why this picture is so important: Jesus standing in the Jordan, with God the Father in the all-powerful love of the Holy Spirit attesting of Jesus, "You are my Son, whom I love; with you I am well pleased" (Mark 1:11). Jesus is revealed from the outset as God's true Son, and he will accomplish what Israel had been unable to, revealing God and mediating God's saving love to the world. Jesus is not negating what God had done through Israel, but is fulfilling this calling to be God's Son. So, standing in the Jordan River, both Jesus's identity and his mission are revealed in this one statement: "You are my Son." This attestation is the river that nourishes and defines Jesus's soul.

The Spirit immediately drives Jesus into the wilderness where, for forty days, he fasts and prays and is tempted by the devil. He symbolically re-lives Israel's forty years of wandering in the wilderness. However, unlike Israel's faithlessness in demanding food, testing and doubting God, and worshipping a creature instead of the Creator (see Exodus chapters 16, 17, and 32), Jesus refuses each of these temptations—refuses to demand bread, refuses to test God, refuses to worship a creature (Matt 4:1–11). He remains faithful through temptation because he is nourished and defined by God, nothing else. He is connected to the source and his soul runs deep and healthy.

It's at this point that Jesus begins his ministry, sounding and living the call: "God's kingdom rule is here! Repent and believe this good news! Stop identifying yourself in any way other than as God's children." Jesus was sounding a wakeup call to the soul of his people, and to your soul. Yes, you have a soul. Your soul is your real life. Before you were born, before your most distant ancestors were ever born, you were an idea in the mind of God, who says, "Before I formed you in the womb I knew you" (Jer 1:5). Your soul is your aliveness, your connection to God, the living river that flows from your source and into the person you see in the mirror. If your soul were cut off from God you would dry up and cease to exist. Tragically, that's exactly what we spend much of our lives doing—damming up that river, cutting ourselves off from our source.

But we look at Jesus in the river. Picture him standing there. See John lowering him into the water. Hear the Father's affirming words. The same statement that nourished and defined Jesus's soul is true of you: You are God's beloved child. Just as Jesus was God's Son, so those who are "in Christ" are also God's children. This reality is the river that nourishes and defines your soul.

We look at Jesus in the wilderness. Picture him standing there. See him kneeling in the dirt and scrub, clinging to his life in the Father. Hear him confronting the temptations of the evil one with the unfailing promises of God. You can seek to draw nourishment and definition from the things of this world, damming up your soul in the process. Or you can overcome temptation by daily claiming your identity and mission as God's child.

We look at Jesus proclaiming the good news. Picture him standing there, right where you are. See him walking the streets of your town, visiting the world's cities and power centers. Hear Jesus's wakeup call: "Repent and believe the good news! Come back to your source so you can live, so your soul can grow deep like rivers."

14

Robert Johnson's Deal

I can close my eyes and picture him—kneeling on the dusty crossroads, calling out for mercy, guitar in hand, full moon overhead, hellhounds barking in the distance, and the devil watching from the shadows. The legend says Robert Johnson became king of the delta blues by selling his soul to the devil. The popular myth tells the story literally. Robert Johnson, a mediocre guitarist, goes out to a Mississippi crossroads at midnight where he meets the devil in the form of a large black man. They make a deal. Robert returns from this meeting with a sudden remarkable guitar-playing ability that can only be described as supernatural. And all it cost him was his soul. His songs like "Cross Road Blues," "Me and the Devil Blues," and "Hellhound On My Trail" were interpreted as Robert singing about his lost soul.

It's fun to romanticize stories like this, and it helps to market an artist when there's a legend around them of mythic proportions. It seems more likely that those who said Robert Johnson "sold his soul to the devil" (a relatively common expression in that culture and time) simply meant he was not a settled-down family man but lived life on the road. Selling his soul to the devil also meant he played secular music instead of religious music. And those songs are more likely about loneliness and alienation than literally being about the devil. Not only was Johnson a black man in the American South in the 1920s and thirties, but he was from a very broken home and had two wives die in childbirth by the time he was twenty-one. I can only imagine how much he felt like a lost soul, like he had hellhounds on his trail. Robert resigned himself to the life of a poor traveling musician and died at the age of twenty-seven, possibly poisoned by a lover's jealous husband. Or maybe the myth is true and he really met the devil out on that crossroad. God only knows . . . well, God and Robert Johnson.

That's the way the Faustian legend goes. Someone sells their soul to the devil in exchange for fame and fortune, but it never turns out the way they think it will. Not only are the fame and fortune not what the person expected, but losing their soul ends up being a bigger deal than they'd anticipated. While this is the stuff of myth and legend, does it have any grounding in reality? Can one really lose one's soul? Jesus seemed to think so. In fact, Jesus seems to have considered it a real threat, to his followers and maybe even to himself.

There was the temptation in the wilderness, where Jesus is tempted to seek fulfillment on his own, apart from God and giving himself over to worldliness and evil. We looked previously at how Jesus overcame temptation by finding fulfillment in his connection to God the Father, his identity and mission as God's Son being the river that nourished and defined Jesus's soul, his real life. We are told that this temptation to seek life apart from God came from Satan, whose name comes from a Hebrew word meaning "the accuser." This seems an appropriate name, but maybe not for the reason we think. We might assume this Satan is called accuser because he accuses us of our despicable deeds. And of course this is painfully true. But just as often we find him accusing God. He accuses God of not being enough and God's ways of being misguided. That's what he was doing to Adam and Eve in the garden, to Jesus in the wilderness, and it's what he's doing to Jesus and his friends in one of their conversations.

First, Peter has a breakthrough. Jesus asks his disciples if they understand what he and his ministry are all about. Peter confesses, "You are the Messiah, the Son of the living God." This insight is major, a bigger supernatural deal even than Robert Johnson's guitar playing. The prophetic confession is so huge, in fact, that Jesus says it didn't come from Peter but really came from God, and it's so important that it will be the foundation of the entire church (Matt 16:13–20).

Then, Peter goes from breakthrough to breakdown. Jesus begins to explain to them that his vocation as Messiah means he must suffer and die, and then he will rise from the dead. Peter pulls Jesus aside and informs him that that is *not* what being the Messiah means, and shame on Jesus for saying such things. Jesus offers his startling rebuke, not only to Peter but also to a figure that seems to be standing behind the poor, misguided fisherman. "Get behind me, Satan!" (Matt 16:21–23). You can almost see Peter looking around and pointing to himself: "Who, me?" Why is Satan, the accuser, being called out here? Because Peter's words are satanic, accusing God of not being enough and God's way of being wrong. Jesus tells him as much, saying that Peter has left God's path and is heading the wrong direction.

Then Jesus expands on this incident with one of his most crucial teachings, and it's all about the soul. The soul, you'll recall, is your real life, the river of aliveness that flows from God the source into the person you see in the mirror. And like a river that gives life and defines boundaries for the people who live near it, so your soul gives you life and defines your boundaries. But also like a river, your soul can be neglected, polluted, and dammed up until it runs dry. That's what Jesus is talking about here: "What good will it be for you to gain the whole world, yet forfeit your soul?" (Matt 16:26—Tellingly, some translations use the word "life" instead of "soul" (NRSV)—in this sense the two words are synonymous.)

The way a crossroads represents a choice to go one way or another, so the cross represents a similar choice: the world or your soul. Which are you willing to give up? You can either stay connected to the source, following its flow no matter where it takes you, what it requires of you, how it changes you. Or you can begin to cut yourself off and go your own way. This cutting off doesn't usually happen in a dramatic moment, making a deal with the devil at a crossroads. It's more typically the result of gradual decisions, like how I define success and what compromises I'm willing to make in exchange for that success; or what qualities of life I'm entitled to and at what expense to others; or what I want others to think of me and what I need to do to cultivate that image; and so on. The stones we use to build such a so-called "life" for ourselves can end up being the very stones that dam up our soul. The life we are building ends up becoming our death. Little by little we gain the world. And little by little we lose our soul.

Jesus isn't only concerned with where your soul goes when you die. Jesus is concerned with your life now, your whole life. Because that's what happens when you neglect and pollute and dam up your soul—you stop being whole. I've mentioned how rivers give life *and* define boundaries. For example, I'm from Texas, which has the Rio Grande as one of its boundaries (which also happens to mark a national boundary). The Rio Grande (along with other boundary lines) serves to integrate the land that constitutes Texas. Boundaries often serve to integrate what is within them. Likewise, the soul is the part of you that integrates the rest of you—your heart, mind, and body.[1] When you neglect the soul, you begin to dis-integrate. Typically your body and its needs and desires take charge and drive the rest. Or maybe you're controlled by unhealthy thoughts or feelings. You find yourself willing one thing, thinking and feeling something else, and behaving still another way. And none of it has anything to do with your identity and mission as a child of God. The river is dry so you have no more definition, no identifying boundaries, nothing that shapes who you are as a person. You might have gained all sorts of worldly things, maybe even become a legend with a sterling reputation and a mythic legacy, but you've lost your real life in the process.

This is a most powerful statement about Jesus's love for you: "Whoever wants to be my disciple must deny themselves and take up their cross and follow me" (Mark 8:34). Some hear these words as harsh. But this is an invitation. Jesus is going to show you the way—he's going to *be* the way—to real life. Jesus is going to connect you to the Father so that the river of aliveness flows in and through you like you never imagined it could. But you can't go God's way and some other way at the same time. And God's way will cost you—perhaps some comfort, some control and power, perhaps the acclaim and approval of others, for some even their physical life.

Those who follow Jesus inevitably end up at a cross, both his and our own. Either we deny ourselves and take up the cross, or we deny the cross and take up ourselves. But whatever it was that was happening to and through Jesus on the cross, it somehow opens the way to the river's source. The way of the cross is the journey of leaving behind all our misguided ideas of power and self-aggrandizement and even life itself, and following Jesus into the life of God. The way of the cross is the way of resurrection. It's the way we must choose because it was the way Jesus chose. The cross is the crossroads. Will we lose our soul there, or will we find it?

---

1. See Willard, *Renovation*, 199. Willard portrays the human self as concentric circles, with the human Spirit (Heart/Will) at the center, and moving outward with the Mind (Thoughts/Feelings) next, followed by the Body, the Social sphere, and finally the Soul as the outermost circle (integrating the others). Ibid., 37.

15

Possessed

Everybody's looking for a sign. But we are surrounded by signs—literal signs. Most of the signs around us are trying to sell us something. And mostly what they are trying to sell us is a way of life. Let's push past billboards and online popup ads. Let's look at the institutions. They're typically associated with some bit of geography, but our lives are the real geography they occupy. Madison Avenue (the advertising industry) is the obvious one: This car or beer or insurance will give you the life you want, the life you deserve. There's also Hollywood (the entertainment industry): This movie or TV show or song or celebrity is all about the life you want, the life you deserve. And there's Washington, DC (the political industry): This candidate or political party or special interest group will give you the life you want, the life you deserve. It could be anything from Wall Street to Walmart to border walls—they're all signs symbolizing some kind of life. And it's the life you want, the life you deserve. Oh, you didn't realize that's the life you want? Well then, first they'll get you hooked on a brand of life, and then they'll sell that life to you. Somewhere out there is the answer. As the saying in advertising goes, "You don't sell the steak, you sell the sizzle."

In Jesus's day it was the religious leaders and the temple system. (Of course in our day we could include some religious leaders and systems as well.) Come to this particular place, buy your sacrificial animal at an inflated price, grease the palms of the religious leaders, and they'll make sure you're right with God. It isn't that this started out as a bad system. Priests and sacrifices and a meeting place were concessions God made in order to help his people relate to him. But it had all become a big, empty sign: These are all the ways you've upset God, and we're the ones who can give you the life you want. God had gotten edged out of the deal. And, needless to say, God wasn't happy about that.

So here's Jesus, living out his identity and his mission as God's true Son. Where the soul of God's people has dried up and begun to die, the river of Jesus's soul remains connected to the source, his unity with the Father in the love of the Holy Spirit. It is through Jesus that life is flowing and definition is clear. And, as typically happens when a river comes rushing into an empty, cracked riverbed, it's a bit overwhelming. Jesus enters the temple, the heart of Israel—Madison Avenue and Hollywood and Washington, DC and the Vatican combined—and he makes a bit of a scene. On fire with prophetic zeal, Jesus stages a demonstration. Picture it: cattle and sheep stampeding, doves flapping, Jesus rushing around with an improvised whip, turning over tables, scattering money all over the floor, running the crooked merchandisers out of the place. And the whole time Jesus is yelling, "Get this junk out of here! This isn't a mall . . . this is my Father's house!"

The religious leaders are upset, not just because Jesus made a scene, but because he tore down their signs. "How are you going to replace our signs?" they demand.

"I am the sign," says Jesus.

"No, the temple is the sign. And you've wrecked it."

"I am the temple," says Jesus.

The world puts up its signs. But each sign turns out to point to another sign. And it all goes nowhere. Even many Christians are looking for a sign. What they ironically and tragically miss is that Jesus is the sign. Sign of what? Jesus is the sign of God's very present authority—God's authority to give life and to govern the life he gives. And so Jesus, more than the Passover sacrifice, more than the temple sacrifices or the temple itself, Jesus is the dwelling place of God—the God who gives and governs life.

And so, for those who deny themselves and take up their cross and follow him, that sign dwells in them, in their soul. And what is that sign in your soul pointing to? God's very present authority to give *you* life and to govern *your* life that he gives. And as the soul integrates the rest of your life—your will, your thoughts and feelings, and your body and its interactions with the world—it is primarily through your soul that God exercises authority to give you whole life and to govern your whole life. It is the Holy Spirit—as much God as the Son and the Father—who does this. Jesus said the Holy Spirit would come to each and all of us, and would teach us everything and remind us of all that Jesus has said, guiding us into all truth and speaking to us the things of God (see John 14:26; 16:13). Basically, through the power of the Holy Spirit, Jesus is a big flashing sign in your soul, pointing to the Father and guiding you into the life of the triune God.

But the choice to bring your soul and, thus, your whole life under God's authority is yours. You have authority over your soul. That's why Jesus says we have the choice between the world and the cross. To deny yourself, take up your cross, and follow Jesus is to accept Jesus as *the* sign, the very presence of God, and to accept God's authority over your real life, your soul. You have to lose your life—to let go of control over it, hand it over to God with no idea what might become of it—to find it.

To choose the world is to choose to keep following their signs, to buy the life they're selling at the expense of your soul. Instead of handing authority of your soul over to the God who gives and governs life, you're selling authority to the highest bidder, to the ones who offer the life that seems most appealing, at least for now. Oh, you might think you have control, but you don't anymore really. That's why so many people are looking for signs, signs of the life they want and deserve. Some even look to popular Christian books and music and celebrity pastors to give them this life. Ideally, such things would be helpful. But they can also be part of a pop-Christian industrial complex that creates a need and then sells the fulfillment of that need.

To choose the world is to choose an external locus of identity, conforming to the expectations of the culture and of others. This is exactly what we see Jesus *not* doing immediately following that dramatic scene in the temple. It's Passover. The holy city is crowded. Everyone's talking about Jesus's miracles and his prophetic demonstration in the temple. He's up in the polls, the press is good, and everyone's impressed. And Jesus doesn't care one bit. He doesn't look to them for his identity and mission because he knows their hearts. They'll be chasing after another sign soon enough. He has already handed the authority of his soul over to the Father. He doesn't need signs. Not only because he *is* the sign, but because the life he wants cannot be bought and sold. The life Jesus wants comes from within. "[M]any believed in his name because they saw the signs that he was doing. But Jesus on his part would not entrust himself to them, because he knew all people and needed no one to testify about anyone; for he himself knew what was in everyone" (John 2:23–25).

What signs are you looking for? What life do you want, do you deserve? Who is the manufacturer or entertainer or politician who will give it to you? Whose approval are you seeking and what are you willing to do to get it? What all of this is asking is, Who possesses your soul? We think of the concept of someone's soul being possessed as the domain of demons and the stuff of movies. But we hand control of our souls over to one person or another, one cultural institution or another, all the time. We buy the lie that somewhere out there is the life we really want. Like the so-called authorities in Jesus's time, we demand our signs. It's time to look for something else.

"Jesus, I've followed so many signs, and they've led me nowhere. I still don't know the way."

"I am the Way," says Jesus.

"Jesus, I've believed so many lies, I don't know the truth anymore."

"I am the Truth," he says.

"Jesus, they all promise to give me the life I want, the life I deserve. But the river of my soul is drying up. I think I'm dying."

"I am the Life," he says. "If you want to come to the Father, to the source, then come with me."

This life, this born-again, eternal kingdom life is a lifelong proposition, not a one-time decision. It is to begin to hand over your life fully to the Father's authority by following the way of Jesus—the way to the Father, the truth of the Father, and the life and revelation of the Father. To be born again is only the beginning of eternal life. The infant mortality rate among Christian souls is far too high! So many have a "born again experience," and then they're done. Being born again is but the dawning of the light, the first step on a never-ending journey. It is a complete and utter change. The change may come slowly, even painfully, but it must come as you move from the external way of the world and its kingdom of darkness and death to the internal way through the cross and into God's kingdom of light and life.

This was what was so discombobulating to Nicodemus, a religious and community leader who was caught up in the world's sizzle, concerned with power and position (see John 3:1–21). He wanted to talk to Jesus about the young rabbi's signs and give this golden boy a pat on the back. But Jesus told him he needed to pay attention to what the signs are pointing to: the Son of Man lifted up, opening the way of eternal life. But in order to live this life of heaven, the life of the Spirit, Nicodemus would have to become a new creature. Though he was a religious teacher and leader, Nicodemus couldn't wrap his mind around the idea of being born again and experiencing God's life in his own soul. He likely couldn't get on board with the idea that he needed any kind of change in what he perceived as a pretty successful life.

But this is the case for you and me. The change happens in the soul. And as your awareness of your soul is like beholding the tip of an unfathomably deep and expansive iceberg, so you must be completely intentional about, and dedicated to, seeking and experiencing God's life in your soul. The soul is real and it needs attention. The life of the soul is eternal life. And though it is mysterious, it isn't lived accidentally.

Because of the mysterious, seemingly elusive nature of the soul, it must be reached indirectly. This is the case for the spiritual life in general. We cannot attain a life of this perfect and perfecting love by sheer acts of our own will. We are reliant on God's grace and God's power. But we can't just tell our soul, "Soul, start cooperating with God's grace . . . now!" Nor can we tell our hearts, minds, or even our bodies, "Begin living from God's power and for God's purposes. Just do it!" We can't do this directly, but this does not mean there is nothing we can do. Spiritual disciplines are acts we *can* do to enable us to cooperate with God's grace and power, which enable us to do what we *cannot* do merely through our own efforts. As Dallas Willard masterfully explains, "The disciplines are activities of mind and body purposefully undertaken to bring our personality and total being into effective cooperation with the divine order. They enable us more and more to live in a power that is, strictly speaking, beyond us, deriving from the spiritual realm itself . . . "[1]

For example, we don't practice solitude and silence just because people and noise are annoying us. We regularly practice solitude and silence to bring our heart, our will, before God alone in surrender. We don't study the scriptures to know trivia. We regularly study the scriptures to know God, to saturate our minds with God's character and story. We don't fast to lose weight, to punish ourselves, or to prove how super-holy we are. We fast, in essence, to move beyond our bodies by submitting them to God, to experience life derived from more than mere bodily food or pleasures. These and other disciplines have no holiness or spiritual value in themselves. They are means of indirectly reaching and nurturing our souls, our spiritual lives hidden with Christ in God, though embodied in the person you see in the mirror. The disciplines place us before God who, in turn, enables us to live the eternal life being made whole in love.

---

1. Willard, *Disciplines*, 67.

The more practical and obvious result of this born-again, eternal kind of life in the soul is the integration of the other areas of life, pulling all into God's authority and power. Your will and your thinking and feeling and your actions begin to be reoriented in a godly direction. And as you employ these other areas in accessing and experiencing God's life in the soul, so the soul nurtures and quickens these other areas. You commit to following the way of the master, Jesus, and you begin to find wholeness in your life. This is God's kingdom coming within, and as it takes hold, you begin to live it outwardly. And as you do this in the Spirit-filled community called the church and in service of your neighbor, God's kingdom of light and life and love takes hold of the world around you.

Even as your body and mind weaken, as your capacity to exercise your will in the world fades, this reborn eternal soul continues to grow, full of light and life. And as you close your eyes to the world and open your eyes to heaven, you find that you've been living there all along. You've gone to be with the Lord in heaven, yes, but heaven had come to you the moment you chose the way of Jesus. You just keep living the life you'd been living since you were born again—an eternal child of light, a child of the kingdom, a child of the river.

16

The Power of Letting Go, or How to Get Away from a Tiger

When I'd lead chapel at my daughter's Christian elementary school, the custom was for the children to bring an object from home and I'd pick one of their objects and teach a brief message inspired (sometimes very loosely) by the object. One time I picked a stuffed tiger a little girl brought. I shared my version of an old Indian parable about focusing on the present moment: A man left the village he'd been visiting and was walking back to his home village. As he got out of town a tiger spotted him and began to chase him. As the man ran from the tiger, he slipped and fell down a deep ravine. On his way down he saw a branch and grabbed on. There the man hung, a hungry tiger above him and a long fall below him. But right next to him was a bush with plump, ripe berries. He plucked a berry and ate it, and it was the sweetest, juiciest berry he'd ever tasted. The end.

I helped the children understand that, whatever they've feared in the past or might fear about the future, none of those things are happening right now. Right now they're okay, especially because God is with them. And God will always be with them, in every "right now." So don't miss the joys of right now because of the fears of the past or future. However, my nine-year-old daughter (perhaps like you) was not satisfied with the end of the story. "What happened to the man," she asked me later. "Did he die?"

Trying to help her understand the nature of parables, I explained, "Well, that's not really the point of the story."

"Yeah, but I want to know how it ends," she insisted.

I gave in. "It can end however you want it to end. You can have the man climb back up and deal with the tiger. Or maybe he dropped and grabbed another branch. Or maybe he just waited. Whatever you want. So, what do you think?"

Without hesitation she said, "He let go of the branch and fell, but there was a river at the bottom."

"That's great," I said, pleased that she had saved the man. "And where did the river take him? It could be the beginning of a whole new story."

"The river took him home," she said, "where he was going in the first place."

So here we are, back in the river with Jesus. It's where we started our journey of the soul, with Jesus being baptized in the Jordan River and the Father proclaiming Jesus's identity and mission with the words, "This is my beloved Son." That was the beginning of Jesus's ministry, and the river was literal. Now we're nearing the end, and the river is metaphorical.

Jesus is on his way home. But instead of a tiger chasing him, it's Greeks (John 12:20–36). These Greeks are likely God-fearers, non-Jews who worship the Jewish God. They are in town for the Passover festivities and they have heard of Jesus, the wise, miracle-working prophet. Basically what this means is that Jesus's reputation has spread. He's about to break out and go big. So what does he do? Climb up out of the ravine and let the culture make a star out of him? No, Jesus lets go of the branch.

Instead of going big, Jesus is going home. He tells this one-sentence parable: "Unless a grain of wheat falls into the earth and dies, it remains just a single grain; but if it dies, it bears much fruit." And then he spells it out: "Those who love their life lose it, and those who hate their life in this world will keep it for eternal life" (verses 24–25). What he's saying in these last days before he dies is just what we've come to understand him saying all along. The stones we try so hard to mine from this world in order to build our life—money and possessions, power and celebrity, pleasure and desires—these are the very stones that dam up the river of the soul. Real life and fulfillment do not come from following the world's ways and building yourself up. Real life and fulfillment come from following the way of the cross and letting yourself go.

This is the final act of letting go for Jesus, and it isn't easy. Jesus says his soul is troubled. The river of his life flowing from the Father feels like rapids rushing out of control. Should he take some time, take things into his own hands, maybe dam up the river just a little bit and slow things down? No. He remembers the beginning in the Jordan—his identity, his mission: "You are my beloved Son."

Now, near the end, Jesus replies, "Father, glorify your name."

And the Father responds, "I have glorified it, and will glorify it again."

The river is flowing clean and strong, and it will carry Jesus home. But understand, home is not just heaven. Home is the embrace of the Father.

I don't remember being afraid of the dark. I'm sure I went through normal childhood *nyctophobia*, and I certainly have those moments as an adult in which I'm fearful about some unknown noise outside at night or in a dark house. But there's a deeper fear of a deeper dark with which I'm all too familiar.

In his *Ascent of Mt. Carmel*, John of the Cross talks about faith as darkness, and that one who wants to live in union with God must enter the dark.[1] This dark faith is opposed to senses and intellect, which is to say opposed to outward circumstances and our constant struggle to figure out how everything will work out and how we can position ourselves for the best possible outcome. The darkness is required for our faith to grow, for us to learn to live in the eternal now, which is where and when eternal life is lived.

We are afraid of the dark, and that fear of stepping into the unknown is understandable. But the problem, all too often, is the reason for the fear. It isn't only because we know there will be struggle and we must learn to walk by faith rather than by sight. The reason for our fear is that we feel sure we are all alone. Surely there is no one there to lead us into the light. Is there even any light at all?

A great source of stress and unhappiness in the lives of many is the inability to live in the moment, the inability to trust that God is living it with us and that we are not missing out on his will or some better path and greater happiness. This is a pattern for many of us. We abandon one road and another because they lead into darkness. We can't see that circumstances will get better with time and commitment to the journey, that things will happen as they need to if we will continue walking with God and trusting his care for our lives. We just can't believe that God is there and is our Father and friend, willing our good.

---

1. See John of the Cross, *Works*.

THE POWER OF LETTING GO, OR HOW TO GET AWAY FROM A TIGER

It is this absence of faith—our misguided reaction to this feeling of aloneness—that has us exhausted and joyless. It is a deep soul-exhaustion because there is no joy in anything at that point. Nothing is good enough. There are no blessings. We are sure we are outside of God's will. So we grasp at phantoms. It is all akin to a spiral of death: sin (seeking life apart from God) results in dying (separation from God), and confrontation with this dying drives us to continue in sin, and onward and downward we go.

And all of this results in a tragic irony: Seeking to flee this feeling of aloneness, we make ourselves truly alone. We exile ourselves from God's grace. We flee the darkness, slapping away God's all-sufficient strength as it urges us on in our weakness (see 2 Cor 12:9). We take on the running of our lives and the world around us, resisting the easy burden of Jesus's yoke. We leave Jesus's path untried, straining against his pace, looking backward and side-to-side—looking for something better, something brighter, something else.

But Jesus walks gently and steadily in the midst of our daily lives and among the ruins of the world he still holds together (see Col 1:15–17), the world he is redeeming. He invites us to get in step with him, to commit ourselves to his way. But it's a way of surrender, of letting go of control and the need to know how everything is and will be. The way of Jesus must ultimately yield to the dark. That's where God is. If we want to walk with God, we must walk into the dark. Only then can we eventually break on through to the other side, where we learn that God "dwells in unapproachable light" (1 Tim 6:16). Greater revelations of God will come, and they will blind us. Yet those who wish to see must choose to become blind (John 9:39).

But God is there. The divine daddy who knelt before us with arms outstretched as we took our first steps, the daddy who stepped back and back as we swam to him, the daddy who unbeknownst to us had let go of the bike as we sped wobbly along, this same daddy is there in the dark. We don't have to be afraid. But we do have to keep going, keep resting in and sharing in God's love. And somewhere along the way we are perfected in that love. Or that love is perfected in us. Or both. It doesn't matter, really. When it finally happens you aren't even aware of it. You're just living, but living in God's life and love.

So we are coming to know what it means that we who are in Christ are God's beloved children. We are born again from above when we lose our life and hand authority of our soul-life over to God. We begin to live eternal life, life that comes not from following the ways of the world and the approval of others, but from within, from the Father who gives life and who guides and governs the life he gives. We begin to love God with our whole soul, living in every way for God's good. But there's one last crucial question: Where does the river flow from here? How does the story end?

This might be the hardest part. The results of your life are not really up to you. Set your goals, work hard, try to make the world a better place. But in the end, all you really have to show for it is you. Those who are following Jesus must ultimately say, "Father, glorify *your* name." That's the way to a fruitful life: Let go of the branch. What falls into the river is the person you've become along the way—nothing else. So many of the things we think are so important are really just branches we cling to, ways of not letting go. It isn't easy. It may trouble your soul. Jesus let go and the river took him to the cross. It took him into the deep darkness of death. But the river kept flowing. It burst open the tomb and carried the risen Jesus into the new creation. It carried Jesus, in the powerful love of the Holy Spirit, across the ages into the lives of billions of people. And it carried Jesus home, into the Father's embrace . . . where he was going all along.

Where does the river flow from here? You can't know until you let go.

STEPS ON THE JOURNEY

Learning to Love with Your Whole Soul

1. Prayerfully read and consider Matthew 16:13–26. What does this passage have to do with loving God with all your soul? Who do you say Jesus is? If you are a follower of Jesus, what does his identity have to do with you?

2. In what ways did your family or a loved one or mentor affirm you, especially in the context of a community, similar to God's affirmation of his "beloved Son"? Spend some quiet time listening to your heavenly Father affirming you (especially if you never had such affirmation in your life): "_____, you are my beloved child. With you I am well pleased." How can you offer this affirmation to someone in your life and/or community?

3. Name some specific ways people "dam up" their souls, turning to worldly things that end up blocking their connection to God. What are some "stones" that you are using to build your life that could actually end up being obstacles to a full life with God?

4. In what ways do you see your culture encouraging an "external locus of identity," defining life according to sources outside the person? In what ways might this be helpful? In what ways is it harmful? In what ways have you done this?

5. Consider which spiritual disciplines might help you place your life before God. Utilize a resource like Willard's *Spirit of the Disciplines* or Foster's *Celebration of Discipline*. Introduce appropriate disciplines into your life, remembering that their value is in helping us

indirectly reach and nurture our souls and cooperate with God's power and grace.

6. In their weekly small group meetings, early Methodists would ask one another, "How is it with your soul?" It is important to be in a relationship with other disciples in which some form of that question is honestly and regularly asked and answered. Do you have such a relationship? How is it with your soul?

PART V

Neighbors: Walling In or Walling Out

17

Across the Tracks

From around ages five through thirteen I lived in the idyllic small town of Memphis, Texas. It was a railroad town, the cotton capital of the Panhandle, Bob Wills country. My grandparents had each moved there, met, and married in the 1920s, my granddaddy a businessman and my grandmother an English teacher. They raised their five kids there through the 1940s and fifties. And it's where I grew up in the 1970s and early eighties. It was a great place to spend a childhood even though it was a bit past its prime. The heart of town was, of course, the town square, which surrounded the county courthouse. Spots of hometown industry sat on streets that ran like red brick arteries outward to commerce, churches, and post-war houses with ebbing post-war hopes. The streets turned to asphalt and ran out to Highway 287, upon which a generation had begun migrating past cotton and cattle and into the surrounding, growing cities of Amarillo and Lubbock or south to Fort Worth and Dallas.

But there was still a critical mass of salt-of-the-earth citizens. My friends and I rode our bikes all over town. We played football, built go-carts and rafts and tree-houses, and fished down at the creek. There were carnivals and town picnics and parades. Everybody knew everybody, and everybody looked out for everybody. I wouldn't trade my upbringing in Memphis, Texas, for a life anywhere else in the world.

But my town, probably like yours, had a secret—a secret lived right out in the open but never talked about. My idyllic small town was segregated, even in the 1980s. There was a section of town literally across the railroad tracks called Morningside. It was established in the 1920s as a place for black workers in the cotton fields to have homes and a community of their own, away from the white folks. Problem is, it never changed. No African-American lived in the town proper. They all still lived in Morningside. Now

PART V—NEIGHBORS: WALLING IN OR WALLING OUT

I know folks lived fine lives in Morningside, with good families, businesses and restaurants, friends and churches, and so on. I don't mean to suggest everyone envied life on our side of the tracks. But the option wasn't even there. The powers that be liked things the way they were. So, the civil rights victories of the 1960s and seventies were only stories in yellowed copies of the *Memphis Democrat* newspaper. Ronald Reagan's 1980s "morning in America" never dawned in Morningside, Texas.

The institutional racism was still deeply entrenched in small towns and large cities throughout the country when I was a kid. It still is, of course. These matters continue to prove more difficult to overcome than we expect, or maybe just more so than we're willing to address. I have nothing but love for my hometown, though this now includes some tough love. But all I knew back then was that I didn't play with my black classmates after school, on weekends, or in the summertime. They went to their side of the tracks and I stayed on mine.

One of the places this was most prevalent was at Fowlers Private Swimming Pool. I can still recall the large black letters on the high pink wall that hid the pool. I was in my twenties and had been away from my hometown for years before I realized "private" in the name really meant "no blacks allowed." I doubt it was an official policy. It was just understood. (I visited Memphis a few years ago and felt a mixture of sadness and satisfaction upon seeing the old pool overgrown with trees and the large wall fallen to rubble.) There was another pool we often went to—the city pool—where my African-American friends would show up, have a great time splashing and diving, and then quickly leave. Most never stayed entire summer days like we did. They'd come for thirty minutes, maybe an hour, and get gone. I didn't really understand back then why they were in such a hurry. But at least they were welcome at the city pool. Segregation had been illegal for decades by then, but nobody seemed to make a fuss over the "private" swimming pool, or the fractured community around it. That's just the way things were. And aren't those the words that most often keep us—as individuals and as communities—from becoming all we might be: "That's just the way things are."

Jesus pushed against those words and it got him in all kinds of trouble. And it saved the world. And the church, from its beginning, has been called to follow Jesus in pushing against those words. That's just the way things are? Not when God gets hold of them. One of the most striking results of Pentecost is the tearing down of internal and societal walls and the movement toward a new unity in the world, to be led by the church. Picture the scene as the newly-Spirit-filled believers spill from their upper room prayer gathering out onto the Jerusalem streets (Acts 2:1-21). Worshippers are collected from all over the known world, in the holy city for the Pentecost commemoration of Moses receiving the Law. They hear these excited rag-tags ranting about the glorious works of God, simple locals speaking far-flung languages. Something very strange is happening, the likes of which the world has never seen. There is a coming together. The scattering and linguistic division of Babel is undone in the gift of tongues. Gender, age, and class divisions are undone in the fulfilling of Joel's prophecy (2:28-29), as God's Spirit fills men and women, young and old, masters and servants. National borders are eradicated by the wonders of God. Long-standing walls are smashed to rubble.

An essential theme of the new creation that began with Christ and his resurrection, of Pentecost and its resulting new community, and of the Spirit-filled age in which we presently live, is unity—people from all different walks of life coming together at God's initiative. Yet our culture and society are plagued by many prejudices—personal and institutional—that keep us from recognizing the value of others that God sees in them, that God gives them. We build walls. But we contort, distort, and propagandize to avoid answering honestly "what I was walling in or walling out."[1] That's a big problem for all, and especially for many of us who claim to be Christians. The next breath after Jesus's crucial teaching that the greatest commandment is to love God with our whole heart, whole mind, whole strength, and whole soul, is Jesus's teaching that that love, by its very nature, is to be directed toward our neighbors. Who is my neighbor, Jesus is asked. Whoever needs mercy, is his parable-reply. And isn't that everyone? Bingo.

If I were to ask you how important it is for us to share our faith, most good church-going Christians would say "very." It's very important, they would say, for us to help people come into a relationship with Jesus so they go to heaven when they die. But if I were to tell you that one of the single most important ways you share your faith is by tearing down walls of prejudice and segregation and helping all people come together—in the church and in the world—thereby participating in God's kingdom shalom on earth, many would become very uncomfortable and perhaps even angry.

---

1. See Robert Frost, "Mending Wall."

But that is the case. We see in the ongoing ministry of Jesus through the church in the power of the Holy Spirit that there is absolutely no place for prejudice and segregation. Not only is there no place for it, it is sin. It is sinful to judge someone based on their skin color or gender or sexual orientation or ethnicity or social class or nationality or any other classification we think sums up this whole person—usually negatively—so we can build a wall between us and them and have nothing further to do with them. It's sinful because it seeks to categorize and dehumanize someone God made and loves. And it's sinful because God is bringing people together . . . all people. When we are prejudiced and when we segregate we are working against God. If you and I are welcome, then everyone's welcome. We are no more entitled to be part of God's kingdom than anyone else.

We too easily bring our segregated small towns into our faith. We want Christianity to mean everyone is like us and nothing ever changes and we don't have to fear being around someone who is too different. But that's not Jesus's church or plan for the world. That's not what the Holy Spirit is doing in the world. That isn't the Father's family. A church and even a world that feel like a small town are great—generations growing together, a welcoming place for kids, everyone working and singing together, having parades and picnics . . . that's all wonderful. But if it's truly God's church, if it's truly God's kingdom, if it's truly God's world, then when we say everybody looks out for everybody, we mean *everybody*.

The Pentecost story in Acts begins with the words "they were all together in one place," and ends with the words, "All the believers were together and had everything in common . . . " (2:1, 44). And right in the middle is the profound good news from the prophet, Joel, via the preacher, Peter, "And everyone who calls on the name of the Lord will be saved" (2:21, see Joel 2:32). A friend and fellow language lover joked with me one Sunday after I preached a sermon on this passage. He said, "The Hebrew and Greek expression for 'everyone' used in Joel and Acts is very unusual. Do you know what it actually means?" I looked at him in confusion and curiosity. He replied, "It means *everyone*." I imagine each of us needs that clarification for some area of our worldview: everyone means everyone.

If you want to be part of what Jesus is doing, if you want to be part of God's kingdom, if you want to be the church . . . heck, if you simply want to be a follower of Jesus, start tearing down a wall. The best place to start is your own life, with someone you might prefer weren't included in that "everyone." Reach out to someone who is different, maybe even someone who makes you a little uncomfortable. Pray for them. Say something kind. Do something kind. When you're tempted to dismiss them and walk the other way, stop. Remember that they are made in God's image, just like you. Recognize that they are deeply loved by God, just like you. Treat them just like you would like to be treated. And then watch the walls start to crumble.

Then, move on from your own crumbling walls and help others tear theirs down. Help your neighborhood, city, and nation tear down its walls of prejudice and segregation. And watch God's kingdom come as people come together. Watch God's kingdom come *in the very act of* people coming together. This is the small town God is building—the borderless, wall-less, billions-strong small town. In Bono's words, it's "where the streets have no names." It's where there is no "across the tracks."

STEPS ON THE JOURNEY

Tearing Down Walls of Prejudice

1. Can you think of a story (movie, book, etc.) about a person or group being excluded who later are included in the larger group or community? What was their journey like? How did they come to be included?

2. Have you ever experienced prejudice and/or exclusion? What prejudices do you hold (be honest with yourself)? What are the deeper reasons behind the prejudice you've experienced and the prejudices you feel?

3. Read the following Bible passages. For each passage note which walls are coming down and how people are coming together. Who is included in God's work?

    a. Deuteronomy 10:17-19
    b. Matthew 28:18-20
    c. Galatians 3:26-29

4. Pick one of the passages from #3 and make it specific to today's world. Where do you see the same divisions and exclusions today? What can Christians do to tear down those walls?

5. Look for a chance to reach out to someone different, whether someone toward whom you've been prejudiced, or just someone from a different background. Take advantage of the chance to act and speak kindly to them and to welcome them with hospitality. Look for practical ways of expanding your sense of community, such as taking public transportation, shopping for groceries in another part of town,

participating in cultural or civic or recreational activities with people from a different neighborhood and a different background.

18

Royalty

My mother taught special education in our small hometown when I was a kid. Almost all of mom's students were minorities. Some were actually learning disabled, many were just troubled kids, and almost all were living in poverty across the tracks in Morningside. Part of their shared reality in poverty was that they weren't given the privilege of learning how to learn. It's hard to think about things like learning skills and homework when your family is drowning in "payday loans" or being evicted from their home or you don't know if you'll have supper that night.

Our elementary and junior high schools were tall, brick testaments to 1920s educational architecture. By the late 1970s they were showing significant wear. Still, most students walked on polished floors past clean glass trophy cases and sat in sturdy wooden desks. But not the junior high Special Ed students. The powers that be decided to make room for those kids in a classroom in the condemned part of the old school. Seriously. The back section of the school was condemned, the outside doors were locked, and most windows were boarded. But every school day, the kids in the Special Education class entered in the back of the school and walked through the gym to their condemned classroom.

But my mother was with them—and she treated them like royalty. She got to know those kids, invested her life in them. I remember several times when mom (a gentle, divorced, white mother of two) had these students (some of them drug-abusing current or future criminals) all over to our house for lunch. They loved mom dearly and would never allow any harm to come to her. Why did they love her so much? Because she took time to listen to their stories. She believed to her core that they weren't "bad kids" who belonged in the world's condemned corners, but that they were God's children who possessed deep worth. A few years later, when mom became the director of the Gifted and Talented program for an entire school district (a different school district), she didn't treat the middle- and upper-class gifted students any differently than she'd treated the working-class special education students. All had equally valuable stories to live and to learn. And all were royalty.

In the letter he wrote to Christians in the first century, James takes issue with the notion of relegating some to a lesser, "condemned" status. He paints an absurd picture of a worship service in which the well-dressed well-to-do are given their pick of prominent seats, while the poor are told to stand in the back or to sit on the floor at the feet of the wealthy (see Jas 2:1-9). Whether or not this was actually happening in the church (and it's quite possible it was), James exposes the evil mindset that makes this a reality in the everyday lives of believers. It might seem absurd to show such partiality in a worship service where we claim to believe all are equal in the eyes of the Lord. But then to go out and make such distinctions among our neighbors—to give preference to the rich and exclude the poor in our communities—is worse than absurd. James says it is sin (verse 9).

It is sin for several reasons. First, to marginalize is to dehumanize. When we condemn a class of people—whether literally sending them to a condemned classroom or systematically structuring our communities in such a way that they are denied equality, opportunity, and justice—we are saying that they are lesser people, that they don't have the same value as those of a so-called higher class. That supposed belief that all are equal in God's eyes is meaningless in the church if we don't carry it into the world of our everyday lives.

Second, to prefer the wealthy and powerful over the poor and powerless is to choose the way of the world over the way of God. God chose Israel to reveal himself to the world, God says explicitly, not because they were a large and strong nation but because they were small and weak (Deut 7:7). It is God's way throughout scripture to choose the needy and weak to demonstrate God's grace and power. To exalt the wealthy and oppress the poor is the way of pharaoh, the way of Herod and Caesar, the way of Satan when he tempts Jesus to do the same. But it is never the way of God.

And finally, speaking of Jesus . . . Not only is partiality for the wealthy not the *way* of God, it is also not the *revelation* of God. James frames this section with a barbed question: "Do you with your acts of favoritism really believe in our glorious Lord Jesus Christ?" (2:1). There's sort of a loaded double meaning here. One, no human's wealth or finery could ever compare to the matchless worth of the "glorious Lord Jesus." He is the only one worthy of our worship—no one else, no matter how wealthy or powerful. The preferred class of the culture pales in comparison to Jesus. But two, despite the fact that Jesus is the Lord of glory, he revealed himself in poverty. He did not consider his divine status something to be clung to, but he laid aside his exaltation and took the place of a shamed servant. And he said his followers should do the same. It is utter hypocrisy to profess belief in Jesus the humble, suffering servant while kissing up to favorites. It was in Jesus's mission statement from the beginning "to proclaim good news to the poor" (Luke 4:18). If it's not good news for the poor, it's not Jesus's gospel. And what is that good news, for the poor and for all? You are blessed . . . because the Lord is with you.

And so the call comes to us. Not only are we not to show partiality to the wealthy and powerful over the poor and humble, but we are to join Jesus in standing with those who struggle for life's basic necessities and for a place and a voice. We use whatever resources or power we have to join the poor in building community, in moving beyond merely surviving to thriving. We go into the "condemned classrooms" of our communities. We reach out to the condemned lives around us that have been told they don't matter and shown they have less value than others. And we treat them like the royalty they are—children of the king.

STEPS ON THE JOURNEY

Tearing Down Walls of Class

1. What's your favorite "rags-to-riches" story? Why is it often the case in such stories that the person was happier or more "themselves" when they were poorer?

2. In what ways do you see a preference for the wealthy, famous, and powerful in today's culture? In what ways are you tempted to favor such people? Why is this the case?

3. Read the following Bible passages. What is the Lord's attitude toward the poor, and how should his people treat the poor and needy among them?

    a. Isaiah 58:6-10

    b. Matthew 25:31-46

    c. James 2:14-17

4. Pick one of the passages from #3 and replace terms like "the poor" or "the least" with specific examples, specific people or groups, from your world. Where/how do you see the poor marginalized in your community and nation? Be specific. What is at the root of such marginalization?

5. Look for an opportunity to stand with the struggling and needy. Perhaps there's a resource through your church, area schools, or community agencies. Also, take advantage of opportunities to value others, to let them know they are important and loved.

19

The Power of Life, or How to Get Away with Murder

When we were around eleven years old, my cousin and I witnessed a murder. We were playing in the parking lot of his grandfather's car dealership in our small hometown. We heard a loud "Pop!" There was a bus depot next door, so I said it was probably just a bus backfiring. Then we heard two more pops and we knew it wasn't a backfire. We ran the twenty yards or so to the corner and saw a man lying facedown in front of the gas station across the street, a pool of blood expanding around him. We saw another man jump into a car in the alley and take off. We ran back to the car dealership to get help.

Soon we heard the ambulance coming. We stood across the street and watched the paramedic, our family friend who always had a new joke to tell, attend to the man lying on the ground. I will never forget the image of that paramedic looking at his partner and shaking his head. That was my first real exposure to violence and humanity's capacity for brutality. The police did their work, including questioning my cousin and me. We were witnesses. And later we witnessed the gas station owner hosing the blood and brain matter off his lot.

"You killed the author of life, but God raised him from the dead. We are witnesses of this" (Acts 3:15). The big-picture result of the coming of the Holy Spirit is power, specifically power to be witnesses (see Acts 1:8). And this witnessing unites us. But witnesses to what? This sentence sums it up, a summary given by a chief witness, Peter, and taken up and shared by all Christians.

THE POWER OF LIFE, OR HOW TO GET AWAY WITH MURDER

First, "you killed" Jesus. God the Father did not kill his Son. Many Christians get confused about this. Did Jesus know this would happen? Yes. He knew his radical message of a coming and present kingdom of love, mercy, grace, and inclusion—and his power and authority within and over that kingdom—would be a threat to worldly powers that would result in his public execution. And he submitted himself to that death as an act of faith in God and God's kingdom rather than capitulate to the kingdom of the world, of evil, and of human power. Did God allow this killing? Yes. Not only did God not stop it, but God transformed the corrupt killing of God's innocent, only-begotten Son into a condemnation of the powers of evil, sin, and death and to open the way of salvation to all who will follow him. But does this mean God killed Jesus? Absolutely not. We must bear in mind the unity of the Trinity and resist the idea of an ontological separation in God, that God was somehow divided against himself. Jesus's suffering and death were the focal point of satanic, natural, and human evil. We don't look at the cross and say, "This is what God did to Jesus." We look at the cross and say, "This is what our evil did to God."[1]

Next, "God raised" Jesus. We don't look at the cross and say this is what God did to Jesus. But we *do* look at the empty tomb and say *this* is what God did to Jesus. (And both are what God did for us and for creation.) If anyone looks at that clash of kingdoms that resulted in Jesus's execution and is tempted to think, "Maybe Jesus's way of love, mercy, grace, and inclusion is wrong. After all, look at what happened to him," then God raising Jesus from the dead is the final verdict on that clash. Yes, look at what happened to Jesus. He was the suffering servant, the holy and righteous one, faithful to the Father and to God's kingdom to the point of death. And God attested to Jesus and his way by delivering him through that death—and through him delivering all humanity and creation. Turns out the way of Jesus is right. And what is that way? To answer that, one has to ask, Who is this Jesus?

Finally, Jesus is "the author of life." This is the shocking revelation of God in Jesus, perfectly articulated in the contrasts of this sentence: "You killed the author of life, but God raised him from the dead." You kill, but God raises—because God (the Father, Son, and Holy Spirit) is the author

---

1. An attitude of humility before the mystery of Christ on the cross is recommended. Nevertheless, there are many thoughts and theories across history as to what exactly was happening, soteriologically, on the cross. This is beyond the scope of this book. A couple of resources are Baker and Green's *Recovering the Scandal of the Cross*, and Wright's *The Day the Revolution Began*.

of life. Which side are you on? You stand as one among many authors of death. Will you follow the way of the author of life?

Peter and many others literally witnessed these things only a few weeks before. The Spirit now gives them power to confront the world's powers and witness to these things, to witness to the life-giving meaning of Jesus's death, resurrection, and identity as the author of life. But the same Spirit still gives us power to witness to the same things. The way of the world is dominance, destruction, and death. *We still kill.* The way of God is surrender, service, and sacrifice. *God still raises.* And the embodiment of both of these truths is still Jesus, crucified and risen.

That is the reality to which we are witnesses, and which is what unites us: Jesus is the author of life. He is the one who brought all things into being. He is the one who exposed the evil of our way of death. And he is the one who offers a better way, the way of life. There are certainly big ways we witness to these things, in our worldview and politics and the powers with which we align ourselves. And we must carefully and rightly align ourselves with a consistent ethic of life. But Jesus would bring it right into our neighborhoods, into our living rooms. How do you think about others? How do you treat your family, your neighbors, even strangers? Those who cultivate hateful hearts and minds stand in the company of murderers. Those who make peace are the blessed children of God. These peacemakers follow their Father in building the new community of the new creation. They are the tellers of the story still being written by the author of life, and still being told in our daily journey of love.

STEPS ON THE JOURNEY

Tearing Down Walls of Violence

1. Do you tend to think of people as generally good or generally bad? What is the worldview that results in your thinking? What are some specific proofs for each way of thinking of people, good and bad?

2. Is violence ever okay? What are some examples of what some consider acceptable violence in the world? Can we ever reach God's shalom through violent means?

3. Read the following Bible passages. What can you learn about God, God's ways, and God's plans for you, your community, and the world?

    a. Deuteronomy 30:15-20

    b. John 1:1-5

    c. Colossians 3:1-17

4. Read through Colossians 3:1-17 another time or two. Imagine what would happen if people actually lived this way in your church, community, nation, and the world. How can you begin to live this way? Consider what it means that your life is not at the mercy and whims of worldly powers but is safely hidden with Christ in God.

5. What might it look like to value life in all areas of your being (personal, societal, national, global)? Look for ways you can work for life in the midst of violence: work with a group like *International Justice Mission* or *Amnesty International*; advocate for just and non-violent policies in local, state, and national law-making and elections; work with civic and neighborhood groups for peace with justice in your

city, including local schools, churches, and law enforcement; work to overcome your own anger.

20

With God on Our Side

I was named after my grandfather. My big brother was named after our great-grandfather, as well as our uncle. But my brother, John, and I were also named after John and Robert Kennedy, which is telling. Our parents could be described as hippies, I suppose, but the slightly older, intellectual type of hippies—the kind for whom "peace and love" wasn't just fashionable but was deeply ideological. So our upbringing was often a clash of ideals. We'd spend childhood summers attending "No Nukes" rallies with our dad in Colorado or Washington, DC. And we'd spend the rest of the year in our small Texas hometown in which talk of nuclear disarmament bordered on treason. Our parents exposed us to art and literature and ideas that were alien to most of our friends and their families.

I got sent to the principal's office when I was twelve because the teacher overheard me quoting Richard Wright's short story "Big Boy Leaves Home" (interestingly, in light of chapter 17, a story about a black boy and his friends going to a whites-only swimming hole): "Yo mama don wear no drawers, Ah seena when she pulled em off . . . " and so on.[1] It's understandable that this silly song would upset the teacher. But as I explained that it was from a story by Richard Wright, I expected the teacher to be impressed by my knowledge of literature. She wasn't. The principal wasn't either. Many times I discovered the hard way that most of my fellow citizens weren't really interested in what I knew, especially from the realm of arts and culture, and more especially when it ran against the prevailing ideology.

I tried to adapt. I joined 4-H and was on the livestock judging team. I raised sheep and showed them at livestock shows. I dipped snuff and relished cursing. And of course, I played football. It was all a blast! But I also held on to my parents' hippie, "peace and love" ideology, learning to keep

---

1. Wright, *Uncle Tom's*, 17.

it to myself and channel it more appropriately. One of the important things this taught me was the ability to hold things in tension (and to keep my mouth shut). This ability has served me well as a pastor, and as a Christian living in twenty-first century America. And it has informed my deepening relationship with God. But it has also made me unnervingly aware of the destructive potential of ideological walls.

It's easy to be lulled into a false sense of our own open-mindedness and humility. It's relatively easy to think of oneself as open-minded and humble when everyone thinks like we do, or at least when those who think a little differently aren't challenging our position as a majority, our sense of rightness, and (let's be honest) our sense of superiority. We often focus on superficial things like dress, musical tastes, speech, hairstyles, and the like, but the real issues are much deeper—they're ideological. What do we think is most important in life and how best to attain that? When our ideals are mostly worldly—money, pleasure, power—it's easy to get caught up in building walls between us and anyone who seems to threaten those ideals. But the problem with many of us Christians is that we are called to a new set of ideals, ideals that tear down walls. Yet we hang on to our old, wall-building ideals, even incorporating them into our faith. We fashion a god in our own image—with *our* politics, *our* tastes, *our* racial and ethnic and national identities—and we keep calling him "Jesus." But there's no room for all these Jesuses. We must choose: God's Son or our own ungodly ideological offspring.

Peter is one of the church's first case studies in this growth process. He prides himself on his ideological superiority. He believes the right things, eats the right things, and above all he never associates with the wrong sort of people, namely Gentiles. Peter is utterly convinced God is on his side. That is until God tells him otherwise. Peter has a vision in which God tears down Peter's wall of superficial do's and don'ts. Then God arranges a divine appointment between Peter and one of those filthy, misguided Gentiles. Turns out this Gentile has a name (Cornelius), and he has a job and a family. And most shocking of all, this Gentile has faith in the same God as Peter. Uh oh.

Something has to change. Either Peter is going to have to demonize Cornelius and his people and also construct a false god in Peter's own image. Or Peter is going to have to exchange his old, worldly ideology for a new, godly one. He's going to have to (dunh-dunh-duuuunh!) change.

Thankfully, Peter makes the right choice, gets on board with what God is doing, and teaches us some important lessons about tearing down walls of ideology.

Lesson one: God is not on "your" side. Peter says, "I now realize how true it is that God does not show favoritism" (Acts 10:34). God doesn't dismiss someone or favor someone else because of their political party, nationality or ethnicity, or even because of their religion. Don't get me wrong—this does *not* mean there is no right and wrong. It just means it is God who is right and we must do our best to be on God's side. But even the very idea of "God's side" borders on nonsensical because God is the profoundest mystery. There is right and wrong in relation to God, but there is no "side" really. The best way to say it is, God is God. So the better option is to do our best, with grace and deep humility, to let God be God and to align our lives accordingly.

Lesson two: God is alive and well among the "other" side. Peter and his Jewish companions were "astonished that the gift of the Holy Spirit had been poured out even on Gentiles" (10:45). God loves "them"—whoever "they" may be—and God is actively working for their good. And we are called to join God in love and good works for the "other" in our lives and world. That crazy Jesus commanded his followers even to love their enemies, to will and work for their good.

Lesson three: God is calling all sides to come together in God's new community. When Peter recognized the others' equality to him, he "ordered that they be baptized" (10:48). This doesn't mean that Peter was commanding the Gentiles, but that he was insisting to his fellow "purists" that the Gentiles be included. Baptism is the official holy sacrament of entry into the church community. So the baptism of these Gentiles into the fellowship and discipleship of the Father, Son, and Holy Spirit, is huge! These new members of the family of faith invite Peter to stay with them a few days. It is in this community where the ideological walls really begin to crumble. And, as Peter discovers, it is also where those walls are fortified.

When Peter gets back to Jerusalem, the other Jewish believers are still holding on to their old superficial ideologies. They condemn Peter because he "went into the house of uncircumcised men [Gentiles] and ate with them" (11:3). Peter shares his story, testifying to God's work among the "others," and then he gives the answer that we should always be ready to ask of ourselves and of others: "Who was I to think that I could stand in God's way?"

(11:17). If God loves all people equally and is working for the good of those he loves (i.e. all people), then who are we to try to stand in God's way?

The same thing that happened to Peter inevitably happens to each of us: we face people who think differently. Either we can demonize them and construct a false god in our own image who supports our worldly values and ideologies over theirs. Or we can exchange those worldly, fear-driven ideologies for God's ideology of love, mercy, peace, forgiveness, and "the light of the knowledge of God's glory displayed in the face of Christ" (2 Cor 4:6). God's ideology is about light, not darkness; knowledge, not ignorance; God's glory, not human glory; and the face of Christ, not the camera-ready faces of politicians or celebrities or talking heads hawking the latest cultural wares or culture wars.

To be on God's elusive, mysterious side is to hold in loving tension ideological (and other) divisions like conservative and liberal, black and white, lost and found, gay and straight, rural and urban, Muslim and Christian, Greek and Jew, circumcised and uncircumcised, barbarian and Scythian (the barbarian's barbarian), slave and free, male and female—for all are one in Christ, who is all and in all (see Col 3:11 and Gal 3:28). Simply put, to be on God's side is to love your neighbor. You can't go wrong with that.

STEPS ON THE JOURNEY

Tearing Down Walls of Ideology

1. What do you think and feel about Jesus's command to love all our neighbors, including the natural world? Resonance? Resistance? Hope? Does this feel too soft? Too challenging? Radically inviting?

2. What are some major ideological divides you can think of, the kinds that affect community, national, and global affairs? What is at the root of each of these divides (are they historical, religious, geographical, cultural, generational, etc.)? What could be done to bridge those divides?

3. Read the following Bible passages. What can you learn about God's plan for tearing down ideological walls and creating community?

    a. Isaiah 25:6-8

    b. Luke 10:25-37

    c. Ephesians 2:11-18

4. Read the continuation of Paul's words on unity in Ephesians 4:1-6. Why does he equate "a life worthy of the calling" with "bearing with one another in love"? Why do you think "oneness" in the church is so important to Christ's mission in the world?

5. Think of people (specific names when possible) with an ideology different from yours—political, ethnic, national, religious, or otherwise. Begin a habit of praying for them. Work for their good when possible. Build community with them via shared interests, a common group, a community organization, or simply over a meal.

CONCLUSION

Becoming the Land

I was on one of those walks, one of those discernment walks where you're hoping to hear from God . . . desperate to hear from God. I carried my small Bible with me. I had been reading through Matthew's Gospel. I walked to the park a few blocks from our newly-wed duplex. Jamie and I had been married only a few months. And I was only a few months more than that into something of a vision quest that had led from mystical mountaintop conversations with God to this humble park. I felt like God might be leading me to be a pastor—maybe. Pieces were coming together. That day, sitting at a picnic table in a park in my hometown of Canyon, Texas, I read an important piece of the puzzle: "When [Jesus] saw the crowds, he had compassion on them, because they were harassed and helpless, like sheep without a shepherd" (Matt 9:36).

That verse, set in the context of a description of Jesus's kingdom ministry and followed by his declaration that the Lord wants workers in his harvest field, worked its way into my soul and became part of my calling. To this day, that image of Jesus feeling and showing compassion for the harassed and helpless people in need of a shepherd's leading continues to inform my pastoral vocation. With compassion I work among the "sheep," occasionally helping some to be a little less harassed and helpless as I point them to the Good Shepherd. But over the years, on occasion, I've wondered: *Is that all there is?*

"What is there about the life and teaching of Jesus that speaks most powerfully to you?" That question came to me in a morning quiet time recently. I was spending time with a devotional based on the life and teaching of Ignatius of Loyola and his reflections on the life of Jesus. It's a fair question: What about Jesus's life and teaching is especially meaningful to me? The problem is, I didn't know how to answer it. And this troubled me. I don't think I'd ever tried to answer it really.

I'd progressed from a childhood, "Jesus is my friend who loves me," to that young believer's decision, "Jesus is the way to heaven"; and then the dogmatic, apologetic teen years of, "Jesus is the God-man," to the activist young adult period, "Jesus cares for the poor and needy"; and then, as a pastor, "Jesus is the world's savior and the master to his disciple-apprentices," and as a doctoral student in mystical theology, "Jesus is the bright revelation of the dark mystery of God." All well and good. But what about Jesus's life and teaching speaks most powerfully to me? To *me*? Not to the books or movements I'm currently into? Not to the authors and musicians and preachers and teachers whose work I'm absorbing lately? But to me? Not to the sermon I'm working on or the study I'm preparing or even the book I'm writing? Just me?

I guess it comes back to that first revelation in childhood: Jesus is my friend who loves me. It's the pictures from my first Bible of little children flocking around Jesus and sitting in his lap. And that friendship and love are revealed in Jesus's compassion for me, that *I* am harassed and helpless like a sheep without a shepherd. I had gotten so caught up in being a shepherd, spent so many years in the training and vocation of pastor, that I forgot what it was to be a sheep—if I ever really knew. Now it began to dawn on me: The Lord is *my* shepherd . . .

So Jesus calls me, even me, to be part of his life and teaching, to be part of him. He leads me and teaches me. He tells me his stories about a kingdom, about the heirs of that kingdom, about life in the kingdom as a steward and builder and even as a child of the king. But it's *me* he wants to lead and teach—not some abstract, generic, and even profound movement or thinker or leader. He's interested in me. This is what it is for *Robert* to be loved and to love. This is what *I* need to do to live freely and faithfully, using *my* gifts and personality and passions and desires to follow him and to be his student and his friend. To my surprise, I am only at the beginning—the beginning of the journey through green pastures and still waters and right paths, the journey through the valley of death's shadow and into the presence of my enemies, the journey with anointed head and overflowing cup into the house of the Lord.

I come as a sheep to the Good Shepherd. I come as a child to my friend. It's okay to say it, to believe it, to live it: Jesus loves *me*, this I know.

CONCLUSION

In the fourth century, Gregory of Nyssa wrote about perfection in a way that feels like it could come from a contemporary best-seller on Christian spirituality.

> Since the goal of the virtuous way of life was the very thing we have been seeking . . . it is time for you, noble friend . . . to be known by God and to become his friend. This is true perfection: not to avoid a wicked life because like slaves we servilely fear punishment, nor to do good because we hope for rewards, as if cashing in on the virtuous life by some business-like arrangement. On the contrary, disregarding all those things for which we hope and which have been reserved by promise, we regard falling from God's friendship as the only thing dreadful and we consider becoming God's friend the only thing worthy of honor and desire. This, as I have said, is the perfection of life.[1]

So for Gregory, this perfection is "to be known by God and to become his friend." Christian teachers across the ages have used the image of the progression from servant of God, to friend of God, to son or daughter of God to illustrate different stages of spiritual growth. But what Gregory of Nyssa here considers the "perfection of life" seems a condition even beyond that of son or daughter of God. Of course that stage of sonship or daughterhood is never left behind. But perhaps it's like the way many of us mature and eventually enter into a new stage of friendship with our parents, understanding them better and seeing ourselves more like them as we live as adults in the world together. They are still our parents, but we have come to a point in seeing ourselves that we can begin really to see them, and *vice versa*.

Likewise, we get to a point of integration in our growth with God at which we move beyond only being children of God to being mature friends of God as well. We grow beyond fear of punishment and superficial rule keeping to living and working *with* God. Jesus's command to "Be perfect as your heavenly Father is perfect" (Matt 5:48) is connected to God's command through Moses to his people, "Be holy because I, the Lord your God, am holy" (Lev 19:2b; see also 1 Pet 1:13–16). The Hebrew word for "holy" here (qâdôsh) conveys the idea of being different, consecrated, set apart. It is bound with the image of a sanctuary. Far from our anemic reduction of holiness to do's and don'ts, it is about a complete transformation from the inside out as a result of a dynamic friendship with the

---

1. Gregory of Nyssa, *Moses*, 137.

living God. We could understand the passage as saying, "Live so intimately and completely with God that your whole life—heart, mind, strength, and soul—becomes a sanctuary."

Jesus invites us into a relationship of rabbi and disciple, which in his time included sharing life together so the student could observe and imitate the master. But Jesus moves this relationship even deeper, to intimate friendship, saying, "I have called you friends, for everything I have learned from my Father I have made known to you" (John 15:15). In our unfolding friendship with Jesus, we observe the holiness and perfection of the Father. So we begin to take on this holiness and perfection, because friends share—motives and desires, thoughts and feelings, actions and things . . . life. Does this seem simplistic? Perhaps that's our problem. Maybe we've overcomplicated things. Or maybe the entire journey is so overwhelmingly complicated that our best option is following a simple path in the sublime simplicity of friendship.

Allow me to offer a final image taken from a very early Christian hymn, probably sung by Christians in Syria around the second century. The words describe trees and plants being watered and nurtured and pruned and then flowering and bearing abundant fruit. The hymn continues, characterizing our faithful lives as planted and rooted in the eternal land of God's paradise. And then, these lines: "And I became like the land which blossoms and rejoices in its fruits. And the Lord is like the sun upon the face of the land."[2]

After being so taken with the natural images in this hymn that I thought I simply *must* flee the city and begin farming or at least gardening, the deep truth eventually dawned on me: This is a picture of love's perfection. The true purpose of this heavenly glimpse is for it to become the reality of my soul as it integrates the rest of my life in God's love. I can't force it. This becoming, this fruitfulness, is nothing but growth in God's grace. God prunes. God fills. God nourishes. And God receives the glory. But I can yield more and more of myself until I am fully participating in the life and love and light of God, the delight of paradise forever. I become the land.

---

2. Charlesworth, *Hymnbook*, 32. See also *The Odes Project, Vols. 1 & 2*, a 2008 album of musical settings of many of these Odes of Solomon, written and produced by John Andrew Schreiner and performed by various artists. The quality varies but, overall, is very good. The setting of the one I'm speaking of (Ode 11), entitled "Meditation on Paradise," is especially lovely.

CONCLUSION

In union with the God who is love, I become love—my whole heart, my whole mind, my whole strength, my whole soul, my whole life in this world among all the people and among the natural world. Love isn't a church or community program, a self-help plan, or a method of personal fulfillment with benchmarks and metrics. Love is a way of being . . . *the* way of true and total being. I become love. This is perfection.

Or at least it's a good place to start.

Bibliography

Augustine. *The Trinity (De Trinitate)*, 2nd ed. Translated by Edmund Hill. Hyde Park, NY: New City, 2012.
Baker, Mark D., and Joel B. Green, *Recovering the Scandal of the Cross: Atonement in New Testament and Contemporary Contexts*, 2nd ed. Downers Grove: InterVarsity, 2011.
Bernard of Clairvaux. "Sermons on *The Song of Songs*." In *Bernard of Clairvaux: Selected Works*. Translated by Gillian R. Evans, 207–278. New York: Paulist, 1987.
The Book of Discipline of the United Methodist Church, 2012 ed. Nashville: The United Methodist Publishing House, 2013.
Brueggemann, Walter. *Interpretation: A Bible Commentary for Teaching and Preaching*, Vol. I, *Genesis*. Louisville, KY: Westminster John Knox, 1982.
———. *Theology of the Old Testament: Testimony, Dispute, Advocacy*. Minneapolis, MN: Augsburg Fortress, 1997.
Charlesworth, James. *The First Christian Hymnbook: The Odes of Solomon*. Eugene, OR: Cascade, 2009.
Colon-Emeric, Edgardo A. *Wesley, Aquinas and Christian Perfection: An Ecumenical Dialogue*. Waco, TX: Baylor University Press, 2009.
Foster, Richard J. *Celebration of Discipline*. New York: HarperCollins, 1998.
Ganss, George. *The Spiritual Exercises of Ignatius of Loyola: A Translation and Commentary*. Chicago: Loyola, 1992.
Gregory of Nyssa, *The Life of Moses*. Translated by Abraham Malherbe and Everett Ferguson. New York: Paulist, 1978.
Griffin, Emilie. *Wilderness Time: A Guide for Spiritual Retreat*. New York: HarperOne, 1997.
Harris, Daniel E. *Grace that Grows: A Method of Thought, Life, and Love for All Christians*. Midland, TX: SalvationLife, 2017.
Holladay, William, ed. *A Concise Hebrew and Aramaic Lexicon of the Old Testament*. Grand Rapids: Eerdman's, 1988.
Irenaeus of Lyons, *Against Heresies*, edited by Alexander Roberts and James Donaldson. South Bend, IN: Ex Fontibus, 2012.
Job, Reuben P., and Norman Shawchuck, eds. *A Guide to Prayer for Ministers and Other Servants*. Nashville: Upper Room, 1983.
John of the Cross, *The Collected Works of St. John of the Cross*, rev. ed. Translated by Kieran Kavanaugh and Otilio Rodriguez. Washington, DC: ICS, 1991.

BIBLIOGRAPHY

John of Ruusbroec. *John Ruusbroec: The Spiritual Espousals and Other Works*. Translated by James A. Wiseman. New York: Paulist, 1985.

Johnson, Ben C., and Paul H. Lang. *Time Away: A Guide for Personal Retreat*. Nashville: Upper Room, 2010.

Levison, John R. *Fresh Air: The Holy Spirit for an Inspired Life*. Brewster, MA: Paraclete, 2012.

Lewis, C.S. *Mere Christianity*. New York: Macmillan, 1952.

Marin, Antonio R. *The Theology of Christian Perfection*. Translated by Jordan Aumann. Eugene, OR: Wipf and Stock, 2012.

Martin, James. *The Jesuit Guide to (Almost) Everything: A Spirituality for Real Life*. New York: HarperCollins, 2010.

Moo, Douglas J. *New International Commentary on the New Testament: The Epistle to the Romans*. Grand Rapids: Eerdmans, 1996.

Nouwen, Henri J.M. *The Return of the Prodigal Son: A Story of Homecoming*. New York: Doubleday, 1992.

Oswalt, John. *The New International Commentary on the Old Testament: Isaiah 40-66*. Grand Rapids: Eerdman's, 1998.

Pseudo-Dionysius. *Pseudo-Dionysius: The Complete Works*. Translated by Colm Luibheid. New York: Paulist, 1987.

Teresa of Avila. "The Way of Perfection." In *The Collected Works of St. Teresa of Avila, Vol. 2*. Translated by Kieran Kavanaugh, 13–204. Washington, DC: ICS, 1980.

Turner, Denys. *The Darkness of God: Negativity in Christian Mysticism*. Cambridge: Cambridge University Press, 1995.

Warner, Larry. *Journey with Jesus: Discovering the Spiritual Exercises of Saint Ignatius*. Downers Grove: InterVarsity, 2010.

Wesley, John. *Explanatory Notes Upon the New Testament*. New York: Carlton and Porter, 1754. https://archive.org/details/explanatorynotesoounknuoft

———. *A Plain Account of Christian Perfection*. Kansas City: Beacon Hill, 1966.

———. *A Plain Account of Christian Perfection*, edited by Randy L. Maddox and Paul W. Chilcote. Kansas City: Beacon Hill, 2015.

Willard, Dallas. *Renovation of the Heart: Putting on the Character of Christ*. Colorado Springs: NavPress, 2002.

———. *The Spirit of the Disciplines: Understanding How God Changes Lives*. New York: HarperCollins, 1988.

Wright, N.T. *The Day the Revolution Began: Reconsidering the Meaning of Jesus's Crucifixion*. New York: HarperCollins, 2016.

———. "God, 9/11, the Tsunami, and the New Problem of Evil." *Response: The Seattle Pacific University Magazine* (Summer 2005). http://spu.edu/depts/uc/response/summer2k5/features/evil.asp

———. *The Kingdom New Testament: A Contemporary Translation*. New York: HarperCollins, 2011.

———. *Matthew for Everyone, Part One*. Louisville, KY: Westminster John Knox, 2002.

———. *Surprised By Hope: Rethinking Heaven, the Resurrection, and the Mission of the Church*. New York: HarperCollins, 2008.

Wright, Richard. "Big Boy Leaves Home." In *Uncle Tom's Children*, 16–61. New York: HarperCollins, 2004.

www.ingramcontent.com/pod-product-compliance
Lightning Source LLC
Chambersburg PA
CBHW072145160426
43197CB00012B/2246